INTERMEDIATE
LEVEL 3

Choral Connections

Mixed Voices

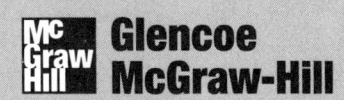

Glencoe McGraw-Hill

New York, New York   Columbus, Ohio   Woodland Hills, California   Peoria, Illinois

Cover Photo: Peter Samuels Photography

Glencoe/McGraw-Hill
A Division of The **McGraw·Hill** *Companies*

Copyright © 1999, 1997 by Glencoe/McGraw-Hill. All rights reserved. Except as permitted under the United States Copyright Act, no part of this publication may be reproduced or distributed in any form or by any means, or stored in a database or retrieval system, without prior written permission from the publisher.

Send all inquiries to
Glencoe/McGraw-Hill
21600 Oxnard Street, Suite 500
Woodland Hills, CA 91367

ISBN 0-02-655613-8 (Student's Edition)
ISBN 0-02-655614-6 (Teacher's Wraparound Edition)

Printed in the United States of America.

2 3 4 5 6 7 8 9   045   05 04 03 02 01 00 99

Meet the Authors

Mollie G. Tower, Senior Author
As Coordinator of Choral and General Music of the Austin Independent School District for 21 years, Mollie Tower was recently nominated as "Administrator of the Year." She is very active in international, national, regional, and state music educators' organizations. Ms. Tower was contributing author, consultant, and reviewer for the elementary textbook programs *Share the Music* and *Music and You*. Senior author of *Música para todos, Primary and Intermediate Dual Language Handbooks for Music Teachers*, she has also written and consulted for many other publications. A longtime advocate for music education, Mollie is a popular clinician who conducts workshops across the country.

Milton Pullen
Professor of Music and Director of Choirs
After attending Texas A & I University where he acquired a Bachelor of Music Education in voice, Milton Pullen attended the University of Houston, where in 1976 he received a Master of Music in conducting. He has taught at the middle and high school levels for 24 years and for the last nine years has taught at the university level. He is now Professor of Music and Director of Choirs at Pepperdine University in Malibu, California.

Ken Steele
Director of Choral Activities
Ken Steele has taught secondary choral music for 23 years, having directed choirs at the middle school and high school levels. He received the Bachelor of Music degree from Stetson University in DeLand, Florida, and went on to the University of Texas in Austin to earn the Master of Music in Choral Literature and Conducting in 1971, studying with Dr. Morris J. Beachy. A member of Texas Music Educators Association, Texas Choral Directors Association, Texas Music Adjudicators Association, and a lifetime member of the American Choral Directors Association, he is currently the director of choral activities at L. C. Anderson High School, in Austin, Texas.

Gloria J. Stephens
Director of Choral Activities
With 25 years of teaching experience, Gloria Stephens is presently the Director of Choral Activities at Ryan High School in Denton, Texas. Mrs. Stephens earned her Bachelor of Music Education and Master of Music Education degrees from the University of North Texas in Denton. She has also done postgraduate work at Texas Woman's University in Denton, the University of Texas at Arlington, and Westminster Choir college in Princeton, New Jersey.

Consulting Author
Dr. Susan Snyder has taught all levels of vocal music over the last 25 years. She holds a B.S. in music education from the University of Connecticut and an M.A. from Montclair State College. She holds a PhD. in curriculum and instruction from the University of Connecticut and advanced professional certificates from Memphis State University and the University of Minnesota. Teaching at Hunter College and City University of New York, Dr. Snyder was coordinating author of the elementary music program, *Share the Music*, and a consultant on *Music and You*. She has published many articles on music education and integrated curriculum and is an active clinician, master teacher, and guest conductor.

Consultants
Choral Music
Stephan P. Barnicle
Choir Director
Simsbury High School
Simsbury, Connecticut

Vocal Development, Music Literacy
Katherine Saltzer Hickey, D.M.A.
University of California at Los Angeles
Los Angeles, California
Choir Director
Pacific Chorale Children's Choruses
Irvine, California

Music History
Dr. Kermit Peters
University of Nebraska at Omaha
College of Fine Arts
Department of Music
Omaha, Nebraska

Contributors/Teacher Reviewers
Dr. Anton Armstrong
Music Director and Conductor, St. Olaf Choir
St. Olaf College
Northfield, Minnesota

Jeanne Julseth-Heinrich
Choir Director
James Madison Middle School
Appleton, Wisconsin

Caroline Lyon
Ethnomusicologist
University of Texas at Austin
Austin, Texas

Caroline Minear
Supervisor
Orange County School District
Orlando, Florida

Judy Roberts
Choir Director
Central Junior High School
Moore, Oklahoma

Dr. A. Byron Smith
Choir Director
Lincoln High School
Tallahassee, Florida

Table of Contents

PREPARATORY MATERIAL — vii

LESSONS

1. Dream a Dream (SATB)   *Ed Robertson* — 2
2. The Road Less Traveled (SAB)   *Carl Strommen* — 11
3. Nginani Na (SATB and soloist)   *Arranger Caroline Lyon* — 21
4. Music, When Soft Voices Die (SATB)   *Philip Young* — 27
5. Cantaremos (SATB)   *Arranger Ramón Noble* — 35
6. Laudate Nomen Domini (SATB)   *Christopher Tye* — 41
7. Pål På Haugen (SATB)   *Arranger Bradley Ellingboe* — 46
8. It Was a Lover and His Lass (SATB)   *Michael Larkin* — 60
9. I Hear a Sky-Born Music (SATB)   *Lois Land* — 69
10. Four Spanish Christmas Carols (SATB)   *Arranger Noé Sánchez* — 75
11. Alleluia (SATB)   *Will James* — 83
12. Flow Gently, Sweet Afton (SATB)   *Arranger John Leavitt* — 91
13. Jesu Dulcis Memoria (SATB)   *Tomás Luis de Victoria* — 98
14. May the Road Rise to Meet You (SATB)   *David Hamilton* — 104
15. In Memoria Aeterna (SATB)   *Antonio Vivaldi* — 111

MAKING HISTORICAL CONNECTIONS

Renaissance Period — 124
  Renaissance Connections — 130
    O Domine Jesu Christe (SATB)
      Giovanni Pierluigi da Palestrina/Arranger Gerald Knight — 132

Baroque Period — 138
  Baroque Connections — 142
  Werfet Panier Auf Im Lande (SATB)   *Georg Philipp Telemann* — 144

Classical Period	**154**
Classical Connections	158
Sanctus (SATB) *Luigi Cherubini/Arranger Patrick Liebergen*	160
Romantic Period	**168**
Romantic Connections	172
If I Should See You All Alone (SAB) *Felix Mendelssohn/Arranger Richard Williamson*	174
Contemporary Period	**180**
Contemporary Connections	186
Still, Still, Still (SATB) *Arranger John Rutter*	188

ADDITIONAL PERFORMANCE SELECTIONS

Shut De Dō (SATB)   *Randy Stonehill/Arranger Mark Hayes*

Warm-Up	194
Literature	197

The River (SATB)   *Garth Brooks and Victoria Shaw/Arranger Carl Strommen*

Warm-Up	194
Literature	204

Look-A That Star (SATB)   *Jay Althouse*

Warm-Up	195
Literature	210

A Holiday Wish (SATB)   *Jay Althouse*

Warm-Up	195
Literature	217

El Progreso Honduras (2-part mixed)   *Elliot Z. Levine*

Warm-Up	196
Literature	223

CHORAL MUSIC TERMS   233

Preparatory Material

Notes and Note Values

1 Whole Note

equals

2 Half Notes

equal

4 Quarter Notes

equal

8 Eighth Notes

equal

16 Sixteenth Notes

Rests and Rest Values

1 Whole Rest

equals

2 Half Rests

equal

4 Quarter Rests

equal

8 Eighth Rests

equal

16 Sixteenth Rests

Rhythm Challenge in 4/4 Meter

Directions: Accurately count and/or perform the following rhythms without stopping!

Asymmetric Meter

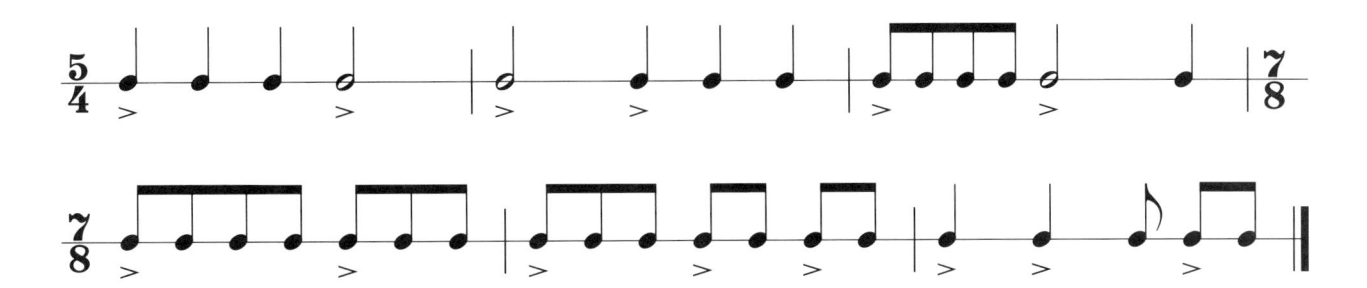

Rhythm Challenge in 6/8 Meter

Directions: Accurately count and/or perform the following rhythms without stopping!

Breathing Mechanics

Singing well requires good breath control. Support for singing comes from correct use of the breathing mechanism. Deep, controlled breathing is needed to sustain long phrases in one breath. Also, correct breathing will support higher, more difficult passages.

Posture
Posture is very important in breath support.
- Keep your body relaxed, but your backbone straight.
- To stretch your back: Bend over and slowly roll your back upward until you are standing straight again. Do this several times.
- Hold your rib cage high, but keep your shoulders low and relaxed.
- Facing front, keep your head level. Imagine you are suspended by a string attached to the very top of your head.
- When you stand, keep your knees relaxed, but do not "lock" them by pushing them all the way back. Keep your feet slightly apart.
- When you sit, keep both feet flat on the floor and sit forward on the edge of your chair.

Inhaling
- Expand the lungs out and down, pushing the diaphragm muscle down.
- Inhale silently without gasping or making any other noise.
- Keep the throat and neck muscles relaxed to maintain a feeling of space in the back of the mouth (picture a reverse megaphone).
- Imagine taking a cool sip of air through a straw, lifting the soft palate.
- Expand your entire waistline, keeping the chest high, and the shoulders relaxed, feeling the breath low in the body.

Breath Control
To help you develop breath control do the following:
- Hold one finger about six inches from your mouth imagining that your finger is a birthday candle. Now blow out a steady stream of air to blow out the flame of the candle.

Summary

STANDING
Feet slightly apart, one slightly forward
Knees relaxed
Backbone straight
Rib cage high
Shoulders low
Head level

SITTING
Feet on the floor
Sit on edge of chair
Backbone straight
Rib cage high
Shoulders low
Head level

Solfège and Hand Signs

Solfège is a system designed to match notes on the staff with specific interval relationships. Hand signs provide additional reinforcement of the pitch relationships.

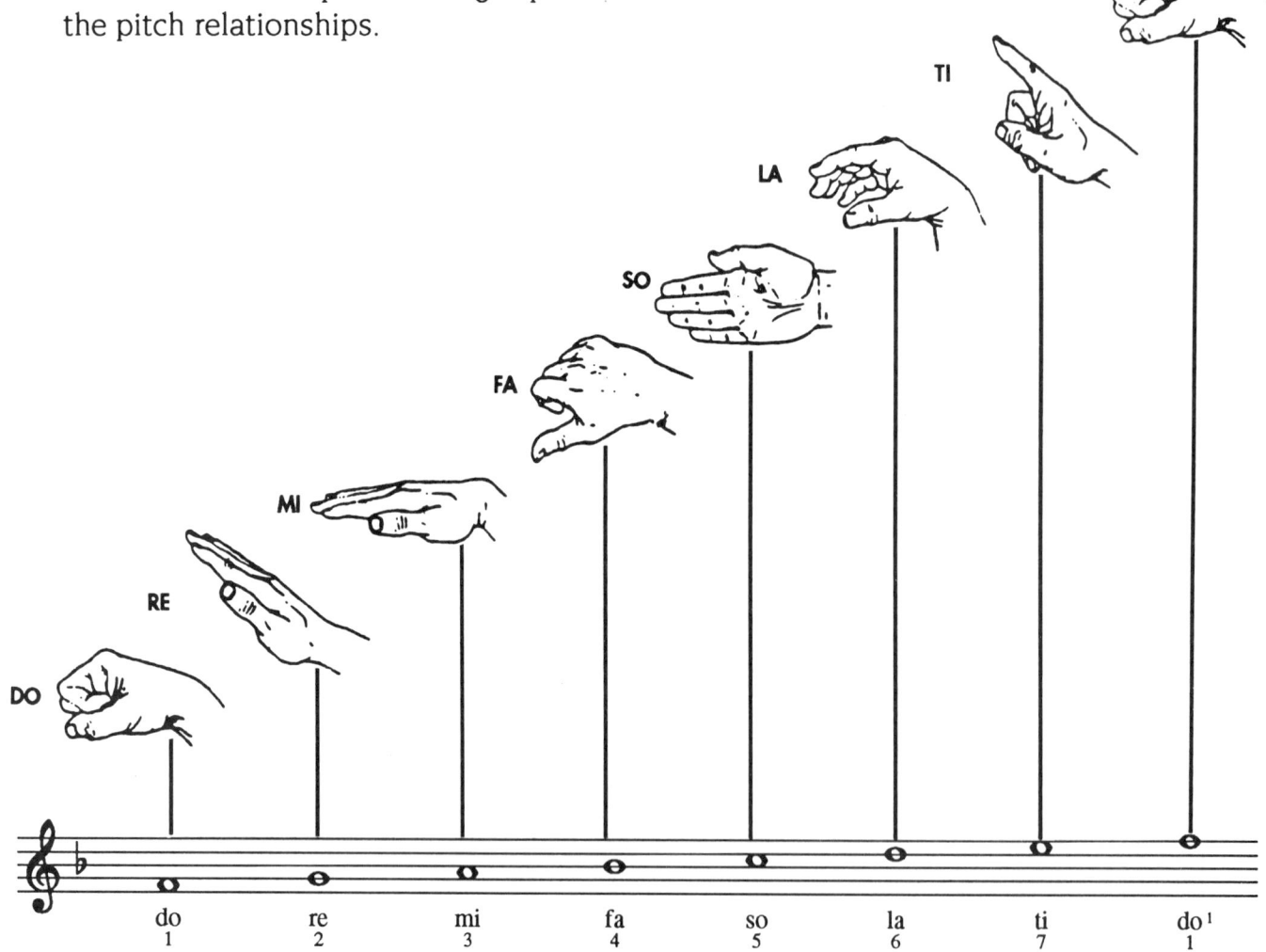

DO¹
TI
LA
SO
FA
MI
RE
DO

do	re	mi	fa	so	la	ti	do¹
1	2	3	4	5	6	7	1

Frequently Found Intervals

An interval is the distance between two notes.

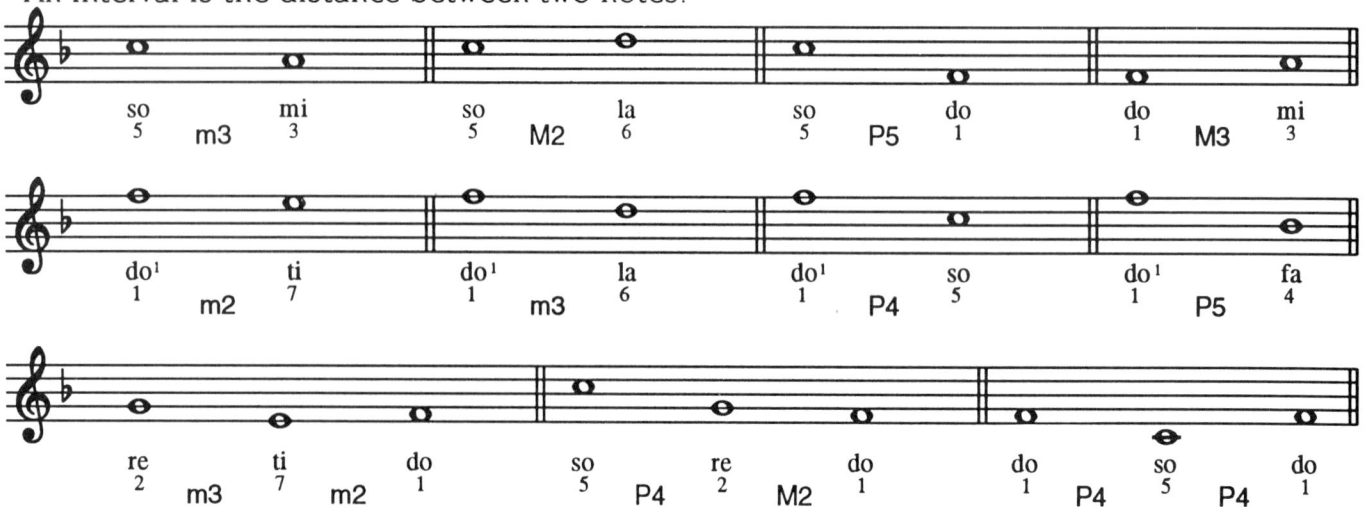

so	mi	so	la	so	do	do	mi
5	3	5	6	5	1	1	3
m3	M2	P5	M3

do¹	ti	do¹	la	do¹	so	do¹	fa
1	7	1	6	1	5	1	4
m2	m3	P4	P5

re	ti	do	so	re	do	do	so	do
2	7	1	5	2	1	1	5	1
m3 m2	P4 M2	P4 P4

Pitch Challenge

Directions: Accurately sing each measure on solfège using hand signs and without stopping!

Lessons

LESSON 1

Dream a Dream

COMPOSER: *Ed Robertson*
TEXT: *Ed Robertson*

CHORAL MUSIC TERMS
altered pitches
breath support
posture
scale tones
syncopation

VOICING
SATB

PERFORMANCE STYLE
Gently
Accompanied by piano

FOCUS
- Read and sing in four parts using proper posture and breathing.
- Recognize and read scale tones and altered pitches.
- Describe and read syncopated rhythms.

Warming Up

Rhythm Drill
Echo these patterns, then clap the whole line with repeats. Take a good breath, and "scat" the rhythm using *doom*, *daka*, and *dah*. You choose when to say which scat syllables—just let it happen naturally. Use one breath for the whole pattern—with repeats!

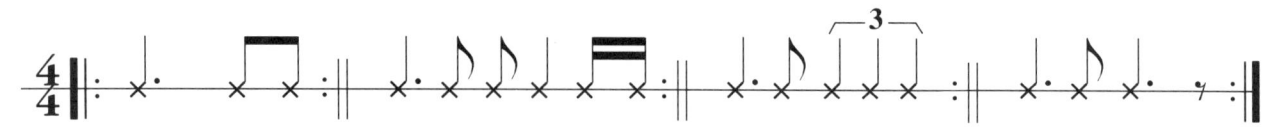

Vocal Warm-Up 1
Sing the scale below using solfège and hand signs or numbers. Now sing one scale tone for each measure of the Rhythm Drill.

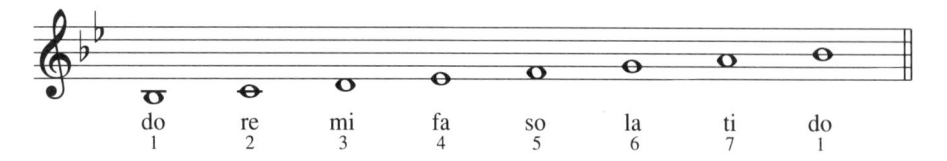

do — re — mi — fa — so — la — ti — do
1   2   3   4   5   6   7   1

Vocal Warm-Up 2
Sing the exercise below on *doo*, *mah*, or other scat syllables. Snap on the offbeats as you repeat the exercise up or down a half step. Notice the altered pitch, and the syncopated rhythm in the last measure of each line. Make it swing gently.

Doo...   mah...

Continue up by half steps.

2 *Choral Connections Level 3 Mixed Voices*

Sight-Singing

First clap the rhythm, then sight-sing this exercise using solfège and hand signs or numbers. Sing each line with one breath. Follow the *da capo al fine*, and *fine* markings.

do so do so mi fa so la ti do mi do so la
1   5 1 5 3 4 5 6 7 1 3 1 5 6

do
1

so te
5 7

so
5

Singing: "Dream a Dream"

People all over the world dream of ways to make things better. Everyone has a choice to work for his or her dreams, and hope that these dreams will come true.

What might you dream for that would make the world a better place? What does Ed Robertson, the composer and lyricist of "Dream a Dream," wish for? Read the text and find out.

Now turn to the music for "Dream a Dream" on page 4.

HOW DID YOU DO?

Dreams take hard work, commitment, and dedication to come true, and so does good singing.

Think about your preparation and performance of "Dream a Dream."
1. What did you learn about posture and breathing in this lesson? Demonstrate good posture and breathing as you sing Warm-Up 1.
2. Sing the B♭ scale again, then tell about the altered tones in "Dream a Dream." What pitches were altered? Choose a part of "Dream a Dream" to sing that will demonstrate that you can sing the altered tones in tune.
3. Describe syncopated rhythm, then clap a few measures to show how it sounds.
4. Is your ensemble able to sing in four parts? How do you sound? How do you know? What is the next step to a better performance?

Lesson 1: Dream a Dream

Dream a Dream

Words and Music by
Ed Robertson

Gently ♩ = ca. 76

1. Dream a dream of a
2. Dream a dream of a

1. Dream a dream of a
2. Dream a dream of a

V 7701

Copyright © 1977 by STUDIO 224, Miami, Florida
International Copyright Secured   Made In U.S.A.   All Rights Reserved
c/o CPP/BELWIN, INC., Miami, Florida 33014

new to-mor-row when the peo-ple learn to love their fel-low
world u-nit-ted when the na-tions choose to lay their wea-pons

new to-mor-row when the peo-ple learn to love their fel-low
world u-nit-ted when the na-tions choose to lay their wea-pons

B

man. Dare to hope for a
down. Dare to hope for a

man. Dare to hope for a
down. Dare to hope for a

Dare to hope for a
Dare to hope for a

Dare to hope for a
Dare to hope for a

Dream a Dream 5

peace - ful morn - ing when we've learned to walk to - geth - er hand in
day of glad - ness when the world can let a smile re - place a

peace - ful morn - ing when we've learned to walk to - geth - er hand in
day of glad - ness when the world can let a smile re - place a

peace - ful morn - ing when we've learned to walk to - geth - er hand in
day of glad - ness when the world can let a smile re - place a

peace - ful morn - ing when we've learned to walk to - geth - er hand in
day of glad - ness when the world can let a smile re - place a

[C]

hand.
frown. If we all will dare to dream

hand.
frown. If we all will dare to dream

hand.
frown. If we all will dare to dream

hand.
frown. If we all will dare to dream

[C]

6 *Choral Connections   Level 3 Mixed Voices*

dreams of a new and bright-er day, if we work to make them come true, we will sure-ly find a way.

true, we will sure-ly find a way.

true, we will sure-ly find a way.

true, we will sure-ly find a way.

decresc.

D

Dream a dream, dare to hope,

of the world we long to see for the day when men are

Dream a dream, dare to hope,

Dream a dream, dare to hope,

Dream a Dream 9

some-day we can see our dreams come true.

some-day we can see our dreams come true.

some-day we can see our dreams come true.

some-day we can see our dreams come true.

slight rit.

10 *Choral Connections Level 3 Mixed Voices*

LESSON 2

The Road Less Traveled

COMPOSER: *Carl Strommen*
TEXT: *Carl Strommen*

CHORAL MUSIC TERMS
intervals
Major 2nd
Major 3rd
Perfect 4th
Perfect 5th
Major 6th
octave
posture

VOICING
SAB

PERFORMANCE STYLE
With feeling
Accompanied by piano

FOCUS
- Identify and use correct singing posture.
- Visually and aurally identify intervals.
- Read, write, and sing intervals of M2, M3, P4, P5, M6, and octave.

Warming Up

Movement Warm-Up
Use your imagination to do this warm-up. *Stand, pretending a birthday cake is balanced on each shoulder. Be sure the cakes don't fall to the ground as you walk carefully around the room, making pathways through shared space.* By doing this, you are demonstrating the correct posture for singing.

Vocal Warm-Up
Sing this exercise using solfège and hand signs or numbers. Then sing it on *loo*, in a legato style. Repeat, moving up by half steps.

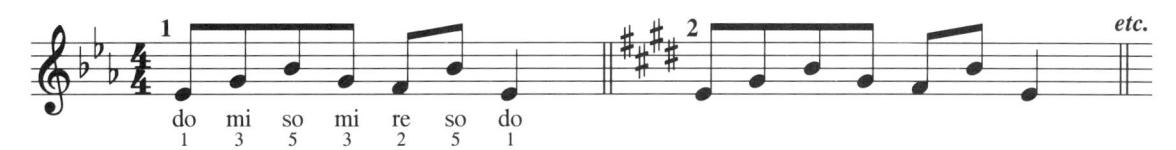

Sight-Singing
Have fun sight-singing this exercise, using solfège and hand signs or numbers. Sing each line by itself. Can you find the stepwise intervals? Thirds? Where is the Perfect 5th?

Lesson 2: *The Road Less Traveled*

Singing: "The Road Less Traveled"

Whether the road is more or less traveled, people usually keep track of how far they have gone. How do they measure distance? What measurement terms do they use?

In music, the term *interval* is used to measure the distance from one pitch to another. You can hear intervals when they are played or sung, and you can see intervals in notation.

Turn to the music for "The Road Less Traveled" on page 13 and find the intervals in measures 2–9.

HOW DID YOU DO?

Think about your preparation and performance of "The Road Less Traveled."

1. Describe how you learned to establish correct posture. Does correct posture help your singing? How?
2. Tell what an interval is, then write the intervals of a Major 2nd, Major 3rd, Perfect 4th, Perfect 5th, Major 6th, and octave, using E♭ as the tonic pitch.
3. Sing the intervals you have written for a partner, and assess each other's accuracy.
4. Describe the intervals in measures 2–9 of "The Road Less Traveled."
5. Is knowing about intervals important for singing well? Defend your answer with a logical point of view.

The Road Less Traveled

Words and Music by
Carl Strommen

SAB Voices and Piano

Lyrics: On that road less trav-eled, plac-es far and wide, on that long and wind-ing road

Also available for S.A.T.B., Level Four (11344), and 2-part/S.S.A., Level Two (11346).
SoundTrax Cassette available (11855).

Copyright © MCMXCIV by Alfred Publishing Co., Inc.
All rights reserved.   Printed in USA.

let your dreams take flight. On that road, that dis-tant road, make the way your own; track-less seas and un-known shores, there are miles to go.

The Road Less Traveled — 15

rain-bow. Hang your hopes on a star.

On that long and wind-ing road, there are miles to go.

Go be-yond the here and now, where you've nev - er

16 *Choral Connections* Level 3 Mixed Voices

been, to that se-cret place you know, where your dreams be-gin. Fare-thee-well and God-speed 'till we meet a-gain. On that dark and wind-ing road

The Road Less Traveled

there are miles to go. Wrap your dreams in a rain-bow. Hang your hopes on a star. On the wings of song I fly to that place so far. Wrap your dreams in a rain-bow. Hang your hopes on a star. On the wings of song I fly to that place so far.

The Road Less Traveled

20 *Choral Connections Level 3 Mixed Voices*

LESSON 3

Nginani Na

Traditional South African Song
ARRANGED BY: Caroline Lyon

VOICING
SATB and soloist

PERFORMANCE STYLE
Swaying
Clapping shaker and drum accompaniment

FOCUS
- Read and sing in 12/8 meter.
- Identify and sing in call-and-response form.
- Sing block chord harmonies.
- Describe and sing using South African vocal tone color.

CHORAL MUSIC TERMS
block chords
call-and-response form
improvisation
12/8 meter
vocal tone color

Warming Up

Rhythm Drill

Perform each line from the bottom up, using body percussion. Feel the sway of 12/8 meter, swaying as you step the bottom line. Divide into four groups and put the four parts together. How does 12/8 meter work?

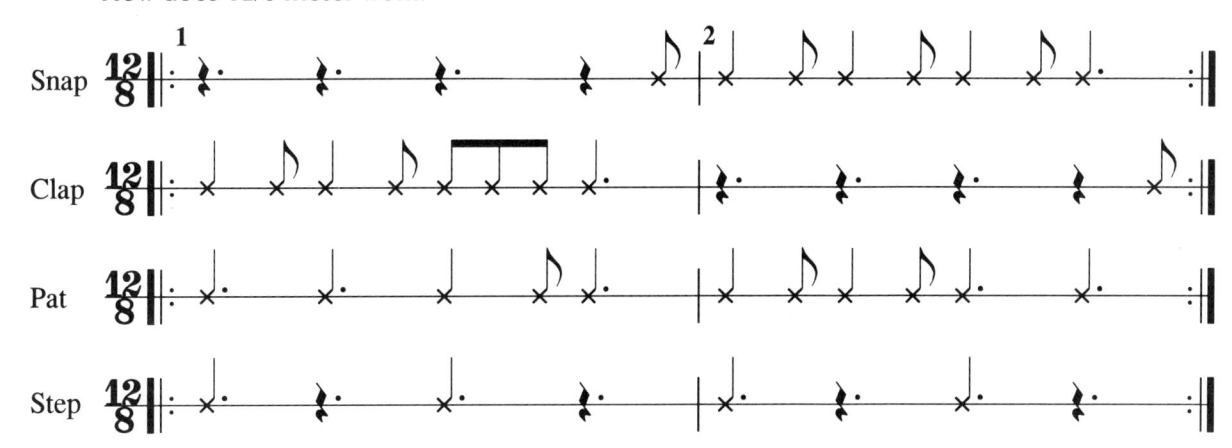

Now echo clap rhythms in 12/8 meter, using the bottom line of this Rhythm Drill as an accompaniment.

Vocal Warm-Up

Sing each "call" using solfège and hand signs or numbers. Then have one person sing each call, with the whole ensemble singing the echo. Sing first on *loo*, then on *nyah*. How is your sound different using these two syllables?

Lesson 3: Nginani Na **21**

In call-and-response form, the ensemble part is not an echo, but an answer. Sing your own answer to each call on *nyah*, using combinations of these pitches: *do, re, mi, so, la,* and *do!*

Sight-Singing

Sight-sing each voice part using solfège and hand signs. Then sing the block chords together slowly. Repeat the exercise, increasing in speed a little each time, until you are swaying slowly as you sing.

Singing: "Nginani Na"

You are going to perform music from South Africa.

Predict what this music might sound like. Make a chart that shows how you think it might be the same as, and different than, pieces you have sung in this ensemble.

Listen to "Nginani Na." After you listen, describe what you heard, and compare it with your predictions.

Now turn to the music for "Nginani Na" on page 23.

HOW DID YOU DO?

Each experience with a new culture helps you understand the similarities and differences that enrich the world.

Think about your preparation and performance of "Nginani Na."

1. Describe 12/8 meter, and clap the Rhythm Drill with three classmates to show your ability to perform in this meter.
2. How is call-and-response form used in "Nginani Na"?
3. What are block chords and where are they found in "Nginani Na"?
4. Describe the characteristics of "Nginani Na," and the characteristics of your performance style that are typical of South African music.
5. If you went to South Africa, do you think all music would sound like "Nginani Na"? What other music might you hear? How could you find out more?

Nginani Na

What do I have? Why am I sick?

Traditional South African
Arranged by Caroline Lyon

SATB and Soloist

Meaning/context:
To be cured in the Sangoma tradition of South Africa, the sick person is being treated by a sangoma (healer). The worried patient thinks, "What do I have?"

Pronunciation:
Solo part: Wuh-meh-meh soon-goh-mah {"z" is allided with the next word} (d)neen-deh-chloh-koh (d)neen-deh-chlah-bah

[Where "(d)" is almost hummed with the lips and teeth parted and the tongue against the hard palate, and where "ch" is like the German sound, passing between the tongue and hard palate with much force and air]

Chorus: (n)dee-yah-goo-lah (n)jee-nah-nee-nah
{the n is silent, but you should still make the shape}

© 1995 Cultural Bridge Choral Innovations

Performance notes:
The soloist may take liberties with her part. The drums should be played with sticks.
Suggested form: A(2x); B (4x); repeat entire song at least one more time.

© 1995 Cultural Bridge Choral Innovations

Nginani Na 25

© 1995 Cultural Bridge Choral Innovations

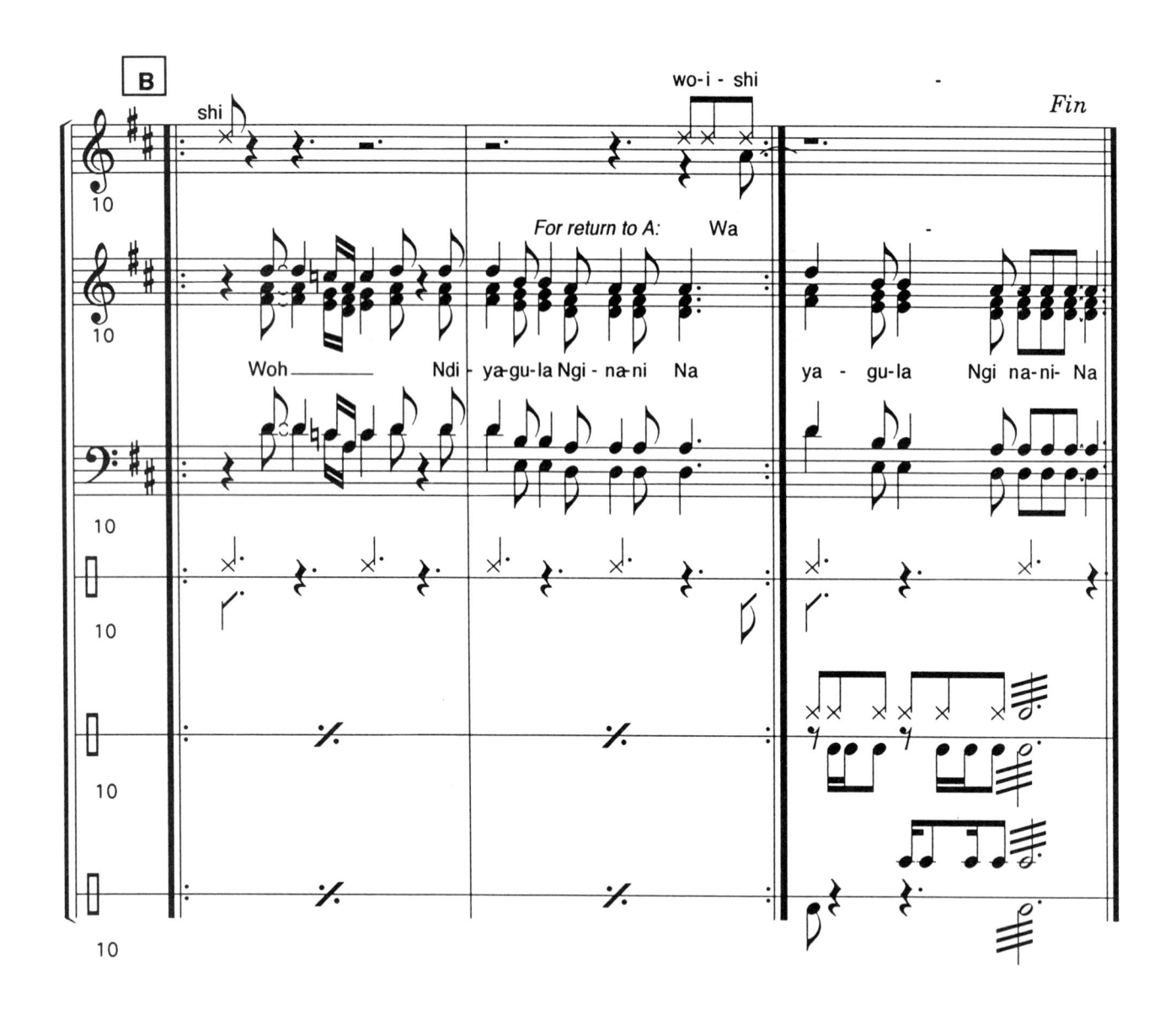

LESSON 4

Music, When Soft Voices Die

COMPOSER: *Philip M. Young*
TEXT: *Percy Bysshe Shelley (1792–1822)*

CHORAL MUSIC TERMS
dynamics
forte
legato
phrase
pianissimo

VOICING
SATB

PERFORMANCE STYLE
Expressively
Accompanied by piano

FOCUS
- Sing legato phrasing.
- Identify and perform dynamics using control.
- Sing in unison and harmony.

Warming Up

Vocal Warm-Up

Sing this exercise following the dynamic markings, creating a crescendo from *pianissimo* to *forte* and back again. Remember to use good posture and breath control.

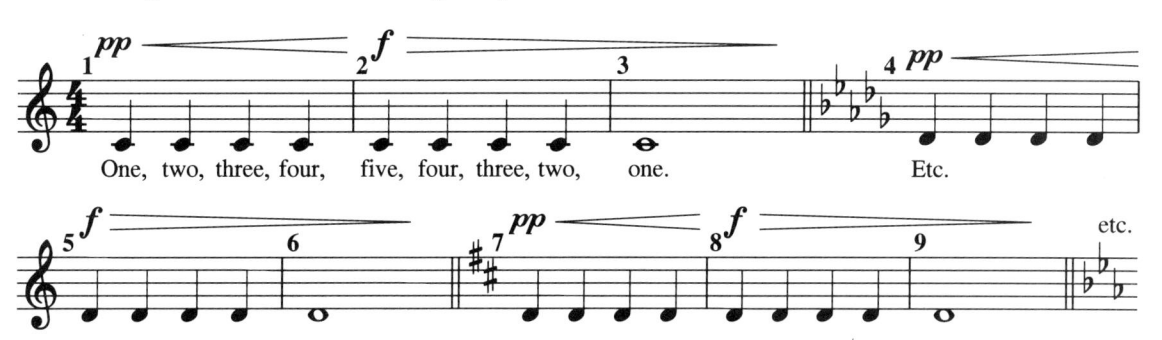

Lesson 4: *Music, When Soft Voices Die* 27

Sight-Singing

Sight-sing this exercise using solfège and hand signs or numbers. Use good breath support, and shape the phrases with appropriate dynamics. Connect each pitch to the next smoothly, in legato style.

Singing: "Music, When Soft Voices Die"

Composers get inspiration from many sources. Sometimes a poem text creates an idea for just the right mood. Read the text of "Music, When Soft Voices Die" on page 29. Phrase by phrase, discuss what the words mean. Then try to communicate the meaning of the poem in one sentence. What musical treatment would you use to convey this meaning if you were the composer?

Now turn to the music for "Music, When Soft Voices Die" on page 29.

HOW DID YOU DO?

The composer, the performer, and the audience make a triangle of musical communication. Think about your preparation and performance of "Music, When Soft Voices Die."

1. As a performer, how did you know where the phrases were in this piece?
2. What did you learn about phrasing, legato singing, and dynamics that helped you interpret the piece?
3. Using the text and notation, describe what effect the use of unison and harmony had in this piece?
4. If you were going to grade the composer on interpretation of the poem, what grade would you assign? Give specific examples and reasons for your decision.

28 *Choral Connections Level 3 Mixed Voices*

For the Choir of the First Baptist Church, Henderson, NC

Music, When Soft Voices Die

Music by Philip M. Young
Poem by Percy Bysshe Shelley

SATB with Piano Accompaniment

30 *Choral Connections   Level 3 Mixed Voices*

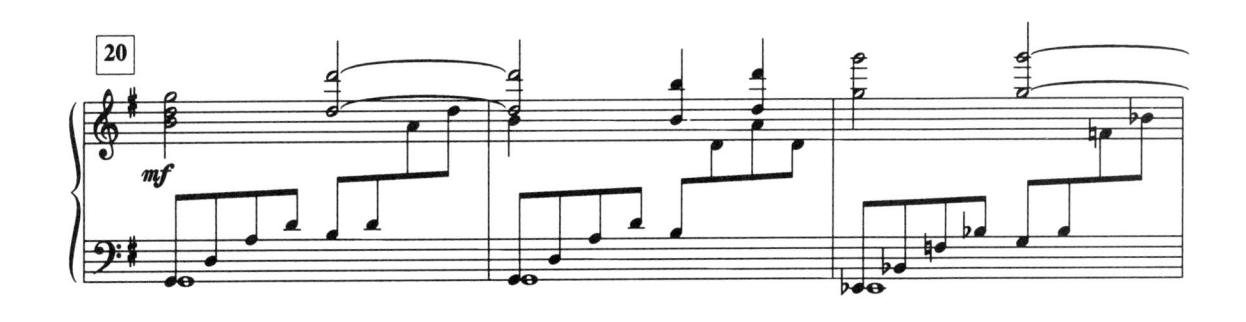

Music, When Soft Voices Die

rose leaves, rose leaves, when the
rose leaves, rose leaves, when the
are heaped for my be - lov - ed's bed; when the
p
Rose leaves,
rose is dead, are heaped for my be - lov - ed's bed;
rose is dead, are heaped for my be - lov - ed's bed;
rose is dead, are heaped for my be - lov - ed's bed;
rose leaves are heaped for my be - lov - ed's bed;

35
S
A
T
B
mf
mp
And so thy thoughts, when thou art
gone, when thou art gone,
p
when thou art gone,
pp

34 *Choral Connections   Level 3 Mixed Voices*

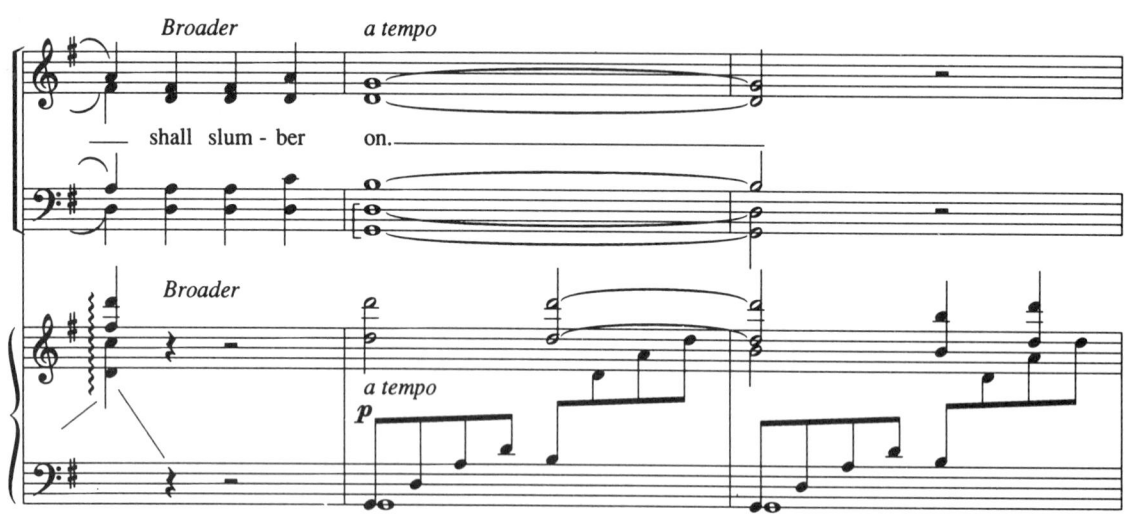

LESSON 5

Cantaremos

Traditional Spanish Dance
ADAPTED BY: *Ramón Noble*
ARRANGER: *Ramón Noble*

CHORAL MUSIC TERMS
AB form
ABA form
a cappella
introduction
rhythm
rondo form
skipwise melodic movement
stepwise melodic movement

VOICING
SATB

PERFORMANCE STYLE
Very fast
A cappella

FOCUS
- Identify ABA form.
- Read and clap simple rhythms in 2/4 meter.
- Identify, read, and sing stepwise and skipwise melodic movement.

Warming Up

Vocal Warm-Up 1
Sing the melody of "Happy Birthday," on the consonant *fff*. Hold one hand on your stomach, and feel your diaphragm controlling your breath.

Vocal Warm-Up 2
Sing this exercise using solfège and hand signs or numbers, then sing again on *ta*. Repeat, moving up by half steps. The *t* sound should help "wake up your breathing." Repeat once more using *loo*, keeping the same feeling of breath support. Notice the syncopated rhythm.

Sight-Singing

Sight-sing this exercise using solfège and hand signs or numbers. Notice the intervals that stay the same, move stepwise, and skip. Clap the B section rhythm. Combine these to create an ABA form.

Singing: "Cantaremos"

Think of the form of some object. Describe the form, without using the name. Can your classmates guess the object from your description?

Form is the organizing shape of something. In music, the form of a piece describes how many sections there are, in what order they are heard, and which are the same. Beginning with the letter A, each new idea is assigned the next letter of the alphabet. Some common forms are AB—binary form, ABA—ternary form, and ABACABA—rondo form.

Now turn to the music for "Cantaremos" on page 37. What is the form of "Cantaremos"?

HOW DID YOU DO?

Just as "Cantaremos" had a form which unfolded, so did your learning as you worked through this lesson.

Think about your preparation and performance of "Cantaremos."

1. As you read the piece, what rhythms and melodic patterns were easy for you? Which need more work?

2. Clap the rhythm of the B section in the Sight-Singing exercise, then make up your own eight-measure rhythm in 2/4 meter, showing your knowledge of rhythms, repetition, and contrast.

3. Describe melodic steps and skips, then sing a section of your choice from the Warm-Ups or "cantaremos" to show your ability to sing intervals in tune.

4. Describe how form occurs in music, and the form of "Cantaremos." Compare the sections, telling what was musically the same and different.

5. Listen to a taped performance of "Cantaremos" by your ensemble, and critique it. What was good? What needs work? What should you focus on to get better as an ensemble?

36 *Choral Connections   Level 3 Mixed Voices*

Cantaremos

Traditional Spanish Dance
Adapted and Arranged by Ramón Noble

38 *Choral Connections Level 3 Mixed Voices*

Cantaremos **39**

40 *Choral Connections Level 3 Mixed Voices*

LESSON 6

Laudate Nomen Domini

Traditional Latin Text
COMPOSER: *Christopher Tye* (1553)

CHORAL MUSIC TERMS
homophonic
monophonic
polyphonic
texture

VOICING
SATB

PERFORMANCE STYLE
Moderately
Accompanied

FOCUS
- Identify and compare homophonic and polyphonic texture.
- Sing homophonic and polyphonic texture.
- Sight-sing pitches in G major.

Warming Up

Vocal Warm-Up
Sing this exercise using solfège and hand signs or numbers, then sing again on *nah*. Repeat, moving up by half steps. Notice the tonic chord tones.

Sight-Singing
Sight-sing this exercise using solfège and hand signs or numbers. Sing each line separately in unison; then combine, trying different voice parts on each line.

Lesson 6: *Laudate Nomen Domini* **41**

Singing: "Laudate Nomen Domini"

Think texture! Look at different fabrics, and compare their textures. Notice how one is rough, while another is smooth, depending upon the arrangement, size, and quality of the threads.

In music, texture is formed by the vertical and horizontal relationships of pitches.

- Monophony is a single line of melody.
- Homophony is created when there is more than one line and all the lines move at the same time.
- Polyphony is created when there is more than one line and each line has its own melody. The lines intertwine, moving at different times, creating harmony by the overlapping of pitches from each line.

Listen to some musical examples, and identify monophony, homophony, and polyphony.

Now turn to the music for "Laudate Nomen Domini" on page 43. What textures do you think you will find in "Laudate Nomen Domini"?

HOW DID YOU DO?

Think about your preparation and performance of "Laudate Nomen Domini."

1. How well could you sight-sing your part with your own group? Was it different with the whole ensemble? What is getting easy, and what is still difficult? What should you work on?

2. Describe the three musical textures you have learned. Plan a short lecture/demonstration with a small group, using musical examples from the lesson to illustrate each texture.

3. Choose either visual art or movement, and describe how monophony, homophony, and polyphony could be represented in this other art.

42 Choral Connections Level 3 Mixed Voices

Laudate Nomen Domini

Music by
Christopher Tye, 1553
Traditional Latin text

Repeat f
or - tu so - lis us - que ad oc - ca - sum e - jus.
ear - ly morn to set - ting sun, His might on earth pro - claim.
or - tu so - lis us - que ad oc - ca - sum e - jus.
morn to set - ting sun, His might His might on earth pro-claim.
ad oc - ca - sum e - jus, oc - ca - sum e - jus.
sun, His might . . . . . . on earth. His might on earth pro-claim.
or - tu so - lis us - que ad - oc - ca - sum e - jus.
set - ting sun, His might on earth, His might on earth pro - claim.
Repeat f

p
De - cre - ta De - i jus - ta sunt, et cor ex - hi - la -
His laws are just, and glad the heart; He makes His mer - cies
p
De - cre - ta De - i jus - ta sunt, et cor ex - hi - la -
His laws are just, and glad the heart; He makes His mer - cies
p
De - cre - ta De - i jus - ta sunt, et cor ex - hi - la -
His laws are just, and glad the heart; He makes His mer - cies
p
De - cre - ta De - i jus - ta sunt, et cor ex - hi - la -
His laws are just, and glad the heart; He makes His mer - cies
p

Laudate Nomen Domini 45

LESSON 7

Pål På Haugen

Norwegian Folk Tune
ARRANGER: *Bradley Ellingboe*
TRANSLATED BY: *Bradley Ellingboe*

CHORAL MUSIC TERMS
chord
repetition
scale
sequence
tonic
tonic chord

VOICING
SATB

PERFORMANCE STYLE
A cappella

FOCUS
- Recognize, read, and sing the pitches of the tonic chord.
- Identify sequence and repetition within a melodic line.
- Sing using correct Norwegian pronunciation.

Warming Up

Vocal Warm-Up

Sing this exercise using solfège and hand signs or numbers, then on the *neh* syllables. Conduct in 4/4 meter as you sing. Move a half step up or down on each repeat. Notice the five repeated pitches at the beginning of each pattern.

Sight-Singing

Sight-sing the two exercises below using solfège and hand signs or numbers. Sing each line separately in unison, then in these combinations: Soprano and alto sing part I with tenor and bass singing part II; tenor and soprano sing part I with bass and alto singing part II. Notice the tonic chord tones and melodic sequence in part I.

Choral Connections   Level 3 Mixed Voices

Singing: "Pål På Haugen"

Listen to the three notes as given below. Can you name this tune in three notes?

These first three notes make up the tonic chord—*do*, *mi*, and *so*. Many melodies are centered around these three pitches, so if you recognize them, and hear their pitches in your head, they will be guideposts as you sight-sing music.

Now turn to the music for "Pål På Haugen" on page 48.

HOW DID YOU DO?

"Pål På Haugen" is a story of learning from your mistakes, and having courage to go on. When you are learning new things, this song has a good message to remember.

Think about your preparation and performance of "Pål På Haugen."

1. Describe the three syllables that make up the tonic chord. Can you hear these pitches in your head? Why is this important for sight-singing?
2. Tell what melodic sequence is, then sing something from the lesson to demonstrate sequence.
3. Find a place in the piece that has repeated pitches. Notice the text, and tell why it makes sense to have repeated tones at this point in the text.
4. How good is your Norwegian pronunciation? What could be better?
5. If you were to meet the arranger of this folk song, what advice would you give for his next arrangement, based on your feelings about this one? Give specific musical examples to support your ideas.

For Anton Armstrong and the St. Olaf Choir

Pål På Haugen
Paul and His Chickens

Traditional Norwegian
Translated and Arranged by Bradley Ellingboe

SATB, A cappella

Soprano: Pål si - ne hø - no på hau - gen ut - slep - te, hø - nunn så lett o - ver
Paul left his hens on the hill - side to wan - der, light - ly they sprang as if

Alto: Pål si - ne hø - no på hau - gen ut - slep - te, hø - nunn så lett o - ver
Paul left his hens on the hill - side to wan - der, light - ly they sprang as if

Tenor: hø - nunn så lett o - ver
light - ly they sprang as if

Bass: hø - nunn så lett o - ver
light - ly they sprang as if

Keyboard (for rehearsal)

© 1992 Neil A. Kjos Music Company, 4380 Jutland Drive, San Diego, California, 92117
International copyright secured. All rights reserved. Printed in U.S.A.
Warning! The contents of this publication are protected by copyright law. To copy or reproduce them by any method is an infringement of the copyright law. Anyone who reproduces copyrighted matter is subject to substantial penalties and assessments for each infringement.

Used with Permission 1995/96.

Pål På Haugen

50 *Choral Connections Level 3 Mixed Voices*

Pål På Haugen

52 Choral Connections Level 3 Mixed Voices

Pål På Haugen

54 *Choral Connections   Level 3 Mixed Voices*

Pål På Haugen

mor!"
ma!"
mor!"
ma!"
mor!"
ma!"
mf
Boom, boom, boom, boom, boom, boom, boom, boom, boom, boom, boom, boom, boom,
Boom, boom, boom, boom, boom, boom, boom, boom, boom, boom, boom, boom, boom,
mf
mf
Ink - je kan ho ver - pa og ink - je kan ho gå - la,
Nev - er will she ram - ble and nev - er will she scram - ble,
mf
In - kje kan ho ver - pa og in - kje kan ho gå - la,
Nev - er will she ram - ble and nev - er will she scram - ble,
mf

Pål På Haugen

43
pyt," sa'n Pål, "eg æ ink - je ban - gen, "Men
shoot," said Paul, "I'm no long - er fright - ened. "But
Pyt, pyt, pyt, pyt, pyt, pyt, Eg ei ban - gen."
Shoot! shoot, shoot, shoot, shoot, shoot, "I'm not fright - ened."
Pyt, pyt, pyt, pyt, pyt, pyt, Eg ei ban - gen."
Shoot!, shoot, shoot, shoot, shoot, shoot, "I'm not fright - ened."
"Pyt, pyt, pyt, pyt, pyt, pyt, Eg ei ban - gen."
"Shoot, shoot, shoot, shoot, shoot, shoot, I'm not fright - ened."
43
rallentando
pyt," sa'n Pål, "eg æ ink - je ban - gen,
shoot," said Paul, "I'm no long - er fright - ened.
"Men pyt, pyt, pyt, æ in - kje bang - en.
"But shoot, shoot, shoot, no long - er fright - ened.
"Men pyt, pyt, pyt, æ in - kje bang - en.
"But shoot, shoot, shoot, no long - er fright - ened.
"Pyt," sa'n Pål, "eg æ in - kje bang - en.
"Shoot," said Paul, "I'm no long - er fright - ened.
rallentando

Quasi Maestoso e calando

Kjæf - ten og mo - te ha hjæl - pet så man - gen. Eg tør nok vel kom - a heim åt a mor!"
Pluck and cour - age my spir - its have light - ened. Now I can dare to go home to my ma!"

Kjæf - ten og mo - te ha hjæl - pet så man - gen. Eg tør nok vel kom - a heim..." Klukk, klukk!
Pluck and cour - age my spir - its have light - ened. Now I can dare to go home..." Klook, klook!

Kjæf - ten og mo - te ha hjæl - pet så man - gen. Eg tør nok vel kom - a heim..." Klukk, klukk!
Pluck and cour - age my spir - its have light - ened. Now I can dare to go home..." Klook, klook!

Kjæf - ten og mo - te ha hjæl - pet så man - gen. Eg tør nok vel kom - a heim." Klukk, klukk!
Pluck and cour - age my spir - its have light - ened. Now I can dare to go home." Klook, klook!

Pål På Haugen

LESSON 8

It Was a Lover and His Lass

COMPOSER: *Michael Larkin*
TEXT: *William Shakespeare (1564–1616)*

CHORAL MUSIC TERMS
dotted eighth-sixteenth rhythm
madrigal style
scalewise melodic patterns
sixteenth notes

VOICING
SATB

PERFORMANCE STYLE
Playfully
Accompanied by piano

FOCUS
- Read and sing rhythms with sixteenth notes.
- Read and sing scalewise patterns with flexibility.
- Identify and perform in a madrigal style.

Warming Up

Movement Warm-Up

You sing best when you are relaxed. Imitate your teacher or a classmate hanging up a load of laundry on a clothesline. Be sure to include bending to pick clothes out of the basket, stretching up to the clothesline, reaching to get the clothespins out of a bag, and pinning various widths of clothes to the line. Bending and stretching will relax your body.

Vocal Warm-Up

Sing this exercise clearly on *da*. Repeat, moving up by half steps. Feel the sixteenth notes over a steady beat, and keep them even. Notice that the melody moves in scalewise patterns.

Sight-Singing

Remember to keep a good supply of air as you sing this little tune. Sight-sing first using solfège and hand signs or numbers, then try the words. Think about this text, and decide what style characteristics to use.

Come a-way my love and hear the birds sing, come a-way for now it is spring.

60 *Choral Connections Level 3 Mixed Voices*

Singing: "It Was a Lover and His Lass"

You know what attire is correct for different occasions. Picture yourself at a concert, at a football game, and then at your grandparents' wedding anniversary party. Describe your attire at each of these events. Does the style of your clothes match the occasion?

In music, composers sometimes write in a style because it is popular at the time, or they might match the style to the text. During the Renaissance, many poems were written about love. Sometimes they were happy and sometimes sad.

Read the text of the Sight-Singing exercise. What is the mood? What musical style would match? Read the text of "It Was a Lover and His Lass." If it has the same mood as the exercise, use the same style of singing.

Now turn to the music for "It Was a Lover and His Lass" on page 62.

HOW DID YOU DO?

Think about your preparation and performance of "It Was a Lover and His Lass."
1. Describe how sixteenth notes work, then sing a part of the lesson to demonstrate how well you can perform them.
2. Sing the Vocal Warm-Up to show your ability to sing scalewise patterns with flexibility. Tell what you learned in this lesson to help sing these patterns.
3. Discuss the stylistic characteristics of a song composed in madrigal style. Referring to measure numbers, describe where madrigal characteristics are found in "It Was a Lover and His Lass."
4. Tell what you have learned about singing in madrigal style.

It Was a Lover and His Lass

Music by Michael Larkin
Text by William Shakespeare (1564–1616)

SATB, Accompanied

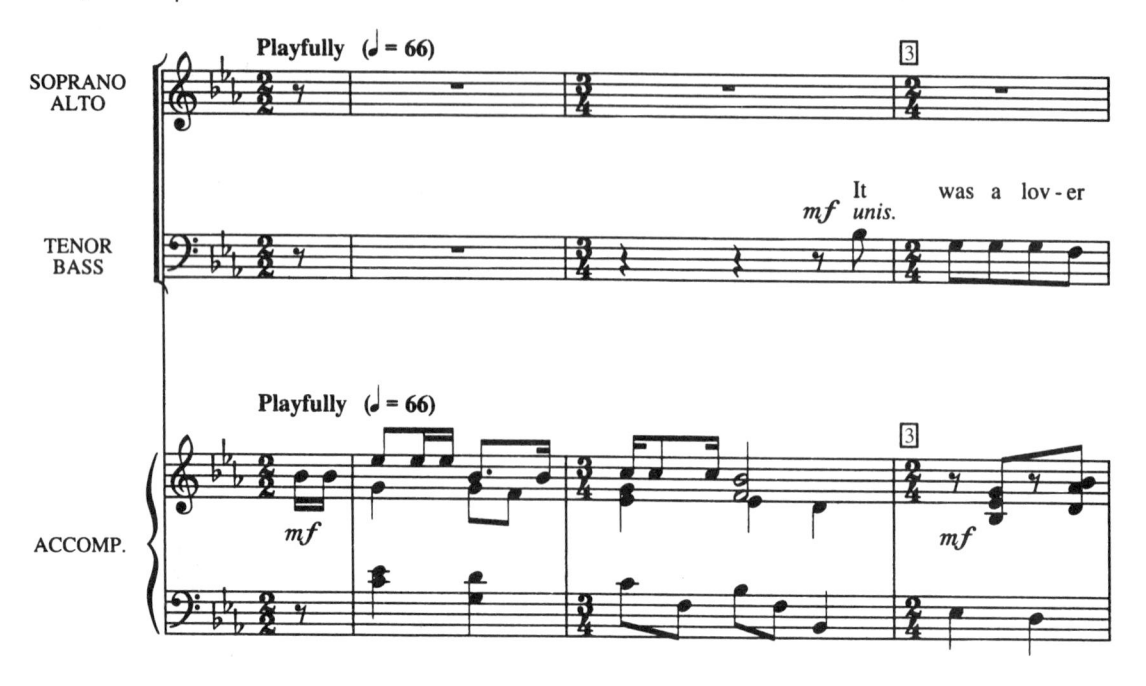

It Was a Lover and His Lass

64 *Choral Connections Level 3 Mixed Voices*

lov - ers love the spring. This car - ol they be - gan to sing with a hey and a ho_ and a hey_ no - ni - no,_ how but a life was but a flow'r in the

spring - time, the on - ly pret - ty ring - time when birds do sing hey
spring - time the
cresc.
poco rit.
f unis.
ding, ding, ding, sweet lov - ers love_ the spring!_ And
ding-a - ding - ding, sweet lov - ers love_ the spring!_
43
a tempo
there - fore take the pre - sent_ time with a hey and a ho and a
f
Take the spring - time with a hey and a ho and a

It Was a Lover and His Lass

WARNER BROS. PUBLICATIONS
15800 N.W. 48th Avenue • Miami, Florida 33014
A Warner Music Group Company

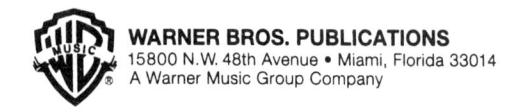

LESSON 9

I Hear a Sky-Born Music

COMPOSER: *Lois Land*
TEXT: *Ralph Waldo Emerson (1803–1882)*

CHORAL MUSIC TERMS
analogy
articulation
dynamics
line
vocal tone color

VOICING
SATB

PERFORMANCE STYLE
Moderate
A cappella

FOCUS
- Identify and select correct vocal tone colors for different songs.
- Demonstrate various combinations of articulation, dynamics, and volume as choices in vocal tone color.
- Describe an analogy between painting a picture and composing, arranging, or performing a piece of music.

Warming Up

Vocal Warm-Up

Sing this exercise on the text provided. Move up or down by a half step on each repeat. Loosen the upper torso of your body as you sing, so it is free of tension. This exercise will help you focus the tone and produce unified vowels. How would you create a purple tone color? light blue? crimson red?

Sight-Singing

Divide into voice part sections and sight-sing your line on page 70, using solfège and hand signs or numbers. Then sing the piece with full ensemble. Discuss places that present problems, and repeat until the pitches are correct. Once you know the pitches, sing the exercise with different dynamics and/or articulation.

Singing: "I Hear a Sky-Born Music"

If you were going to paint a picture, you would need paint, a brush, and canvas. The paint supplies the color, the brush applies the line and color, and the canvas displays the art.

Construct an analogy for the information above that begins this way:

If you were going to compose, arrange, or perform a tone painting, you would need . . .

You will have the chance to paint with sound in "I Hear a Sky-Born Music," by making decisions about color, line, dynamics, and articulation.

Now turn to the music for "I Hear a Sky-Born Music" on page 71.

HOW DID YOU DO?

Just as a painting comes to life color by color and line by line, you have constructed your performance of "I Hear a Sky-Born Music" day by day.

Think about your preparation and performance of "I Hear a Sky-Born Music."

1. Describe vocal tone color, and the process you went through to choose the correct tone color for this piece.

2. What musical elements did you try out in preparing your performance, and how did you make decisions about what was correct?

3. Describe the supplies an artist uses to create a painting, then construct an analogy for these supplies that applies to the process you and the ensemble went through to "paint" your performance of "I Hear a Sky-Born Music."

70 *Choral Connections Level 3 Mixed Voices*

I Hear a Sky-Born Music

Music by Lois Land
Words by Ralph Waldo Emerson

Moderato

S: Let me go where-e'er I will, I hear a sky-born music still; It sounds from all things old, it sounds from all things

A: Let me go where-e'er I will, I hear a sky-born music still; It sounds from all things old, it sounds from all things

T: Let me go where-e'er I will, I hear a sky-born music still; It sounds from all things old, it sounds from all things

B: Let me go where-e'er I will, I hear a sky-born music still; It sounds from all things old, it sounds from all things

Piano for rehearsal only

©Copyright 1988 by Southern Music Company, San Antonio, Texas 78292
International copyright secured. Printed in U.S.A. All rights reserved.

72 *Choral Connections   Level 3 Mixed Voices*

I Hear a Sky-Born Music 73

go where-e'er I will, I hear a sky-born mu - sic, mu - sic still.

74 *Choral Connections   Level 3 Mixed Voices*

LESSON 10

Four Spanish Christmas Carols

CHORAL MUSIC TERMS
meter
Spanish style

Traditional Carols
ARRANGER: Noe Sanchez

VOICING
SATB

PERFORMANCE STYLE
Varied
A cappella

FOCUS
- Sing, using correct Spanish pronunciation.
- Identify and perform characteristic styles of Spanish songs.

Warming Up

Vocal Warm-Up

Sing this warm-up using solfège and hand signs or numbers. Next, sing it once, using a smooth legato *loo*, maintaining accurate, precise rhythms. Then sing it at a faster tempo, using a staccato *deet*. Finally sing it as a four-part canon, starting at two-measure intervals, working for harmonic precision.

Sight-Singing

Sight-sing through all three parts in unison using solfège and hand signs or numbers. Then divide into groups and sing the parts in different combinations, finally singing all three at the same time. Notice the beginning incomplete measures in parts I and II, and the one-beat measure at the end to create a complete measure.

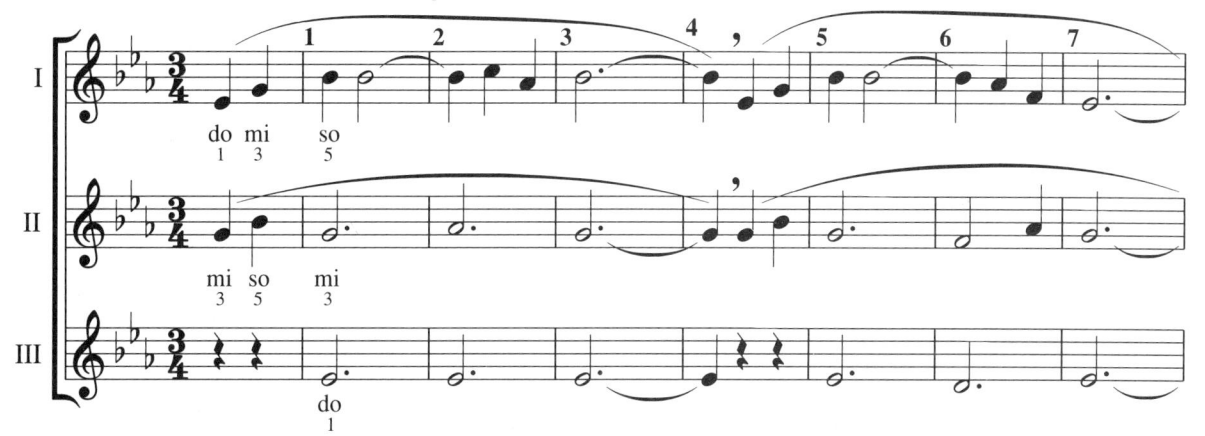

Lesson 10: *Four Spanish Christmas Carols*

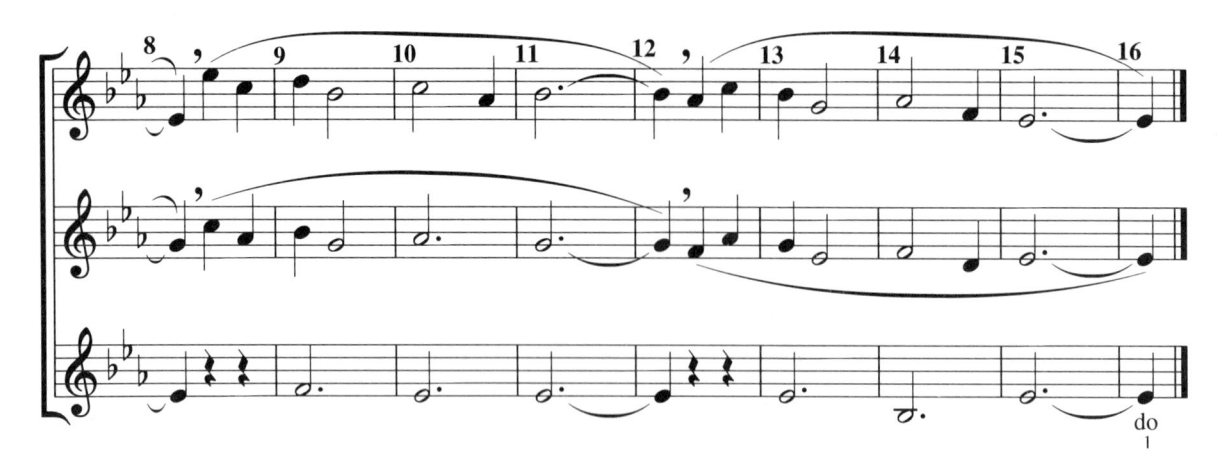

Singing: "Four Spanish Christmas Carols"

These four carols come from Puerto Rico, Spain, and Catalonia (a region of northeastern Spain). They all reflect the Spanish musical style.

Based on your current knowledge of Spanish musical style, predict what musical characteristics you think will make a song sound like it reflects this style.

Listen to "Alegria, Alegria, Alegria," and check it against your predictions. Listen again to add some new ideas based on what you have heard. Then compare your predictions, and the new information, as you listen to "El desembre congelat," "Soy un pobre pastorcito," and "Vamos todos a Belén."

Now turn to the music for "Four Spanish Christmas Carols" on page 77.

HOW DID YOU DO?

To learn about the characteristics of any style of music, you begin with your own knowledge, collect more ideas through listening and reading, and then adjust your original idea based on new information.

Think about your preparation and performance of "Four Spanish Christmas Carols."

1. Is it easy or difficult to sing in Spanish? What is the most difficult? What do you do well?
2. Give a broad definition of characteristics of Spanish musical style, then compare the characteristics of each of the "Four Spanish Christmas Carols," telling how they match the characteristics, and how they are unique to themselves.
3. How would you know if a new song was in a Spanish musical style?
4. Do you think it is appropriate to make general characteristics for the songs of a whole culture? Why? Why not? Give specific examples to support your argument.

Four Spanish Christmas Carols
Alegria, Alegria, Alegria

Traditional Puerto Rican Carol
Arranged by Noe Sanchez

SATB Voices, A cappella

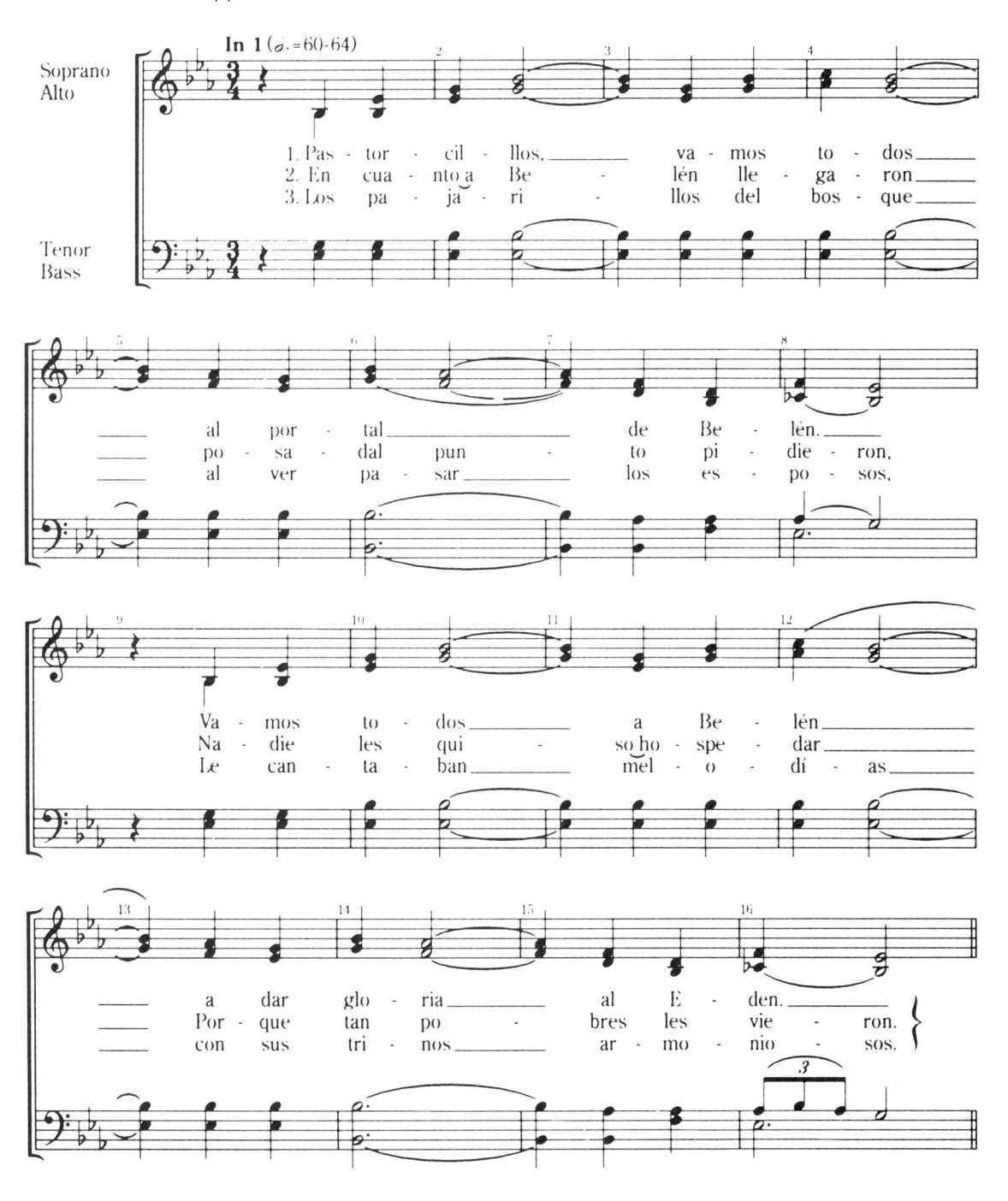

1. Pas - tor - cil - llos, vamos todos al por - tal de Be - lén. Vamos todos a Be - lén a dar glo - ria al E - den.
2. En cuanto a Be - lén lle - ga - ron po - sa - dal pun - to pi - die - ron, al ver pa - sar los es - po - sos, Na - die les qui - so hos - pe - dar Por - que tan po - bres les vie - ron.
3. Los pa - ja - ri - llos del bos - que Le can - ta - ban me - lo - dí - as con sus tri - nos ar - mo - nio - sos.

Copyright © 1995, AMC Publications
A Division of Alliance Music Publications, Inc.
Houston, Texas
International Copyright Secured   All Rights Reserved

78 *Choral Connections Level 3 Mixed Voices*

El desembre congelat

Traditional Catalonian Carol
Arranged by Noe Sanchez

SATB Voices, A cappella

1. El desembre congelat, confús es retira,
2. El primer pare causà la nit tenebrosa;
3. El mes de maig ha florit, sense ser enca(ca)ra;

A bril de flors coronat,
que a tot el món ofuscá,
un lliri blanc y polit,

*In this carol each verse should be sung slower with the last verse in 4 rather than in 2.

Copyright © 1995, AMC Publications
A Division of Alliance Music Publications, Inc.
Houston, Texas
International Copyright Secured   All Rights Reserved

Four Spanish Christmas Carols

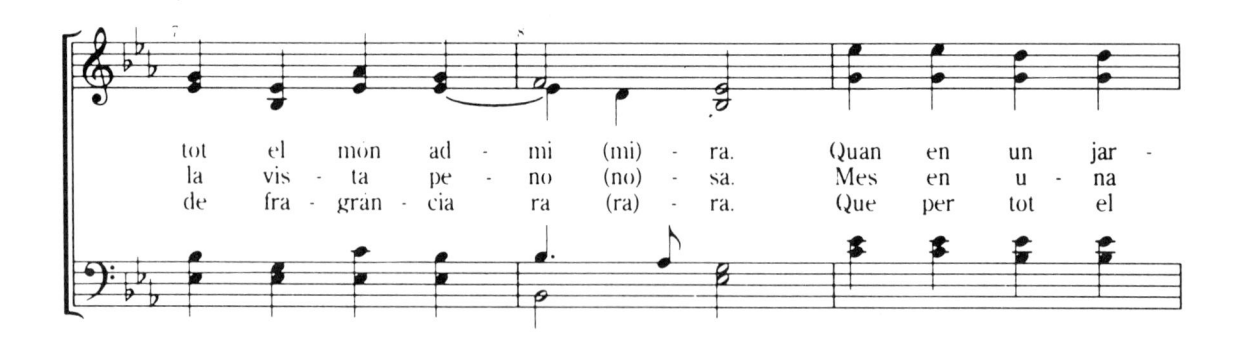

tot el mon ad - mi (mi) - ra. Quan en un jar -
la vis - ta pe - no (no) - sa. Mes en u - na
de fra - grän - cia ra (ra) - ra. Que per tot el

rit.
di d'a - mor neix u - na di - vi - na flor.
mit - ja nit bri - lla el sol que n'és eix - it.
món se sent, de lle - vant fins a po - nent.

a tempo
D'u - na ro ro ro, d'u - na sa sa sa, d'u - na ro, d'u - na
D'u - na bel bel bel, d'u - na la la la, d'u - na bel, d'u - na
To - ta sa sa sa, to - ta dul dul dul, to - ta sa, to - ta

ten. *a tempo*
sa, d'u - na ro - sa be - lla, fe - cun da j pon - ce (ce) - lla.
la, d'u - na be - lla au - ro - ra, que el cel en - a - mo (mo) - ra.
dul, to - ta sa dul - çu - ra, lo - lor, amb ven - tu (tu) - ra.

Soy un pobre pastorcito

SATB Voices, A cappella

Traditional Spanish Carol
Arranged by Noe Sanchez

In 2 (not very slow)

1. Soy un pobre pastorcito que camina hacia Belén voy buscando al que ha nacido Diós con nosotros, Manuel.
2. Aunque soy pobre le llevo un blanquísimo bellón para que le haga su madre un contoncito de algodón.
3. Guardadito a quien el pecho yo le llevo el mejor don; al niñito que ha nacido le llevo mi corazón.

Coro

Caminando camina ligero, no te canses de caminar; que te esperan José y María a con el Niño en el portal.

*If this carol is sung alone (not as part of a set), please end in g minor. If sung in tandem with the following "Vamos todos a Belén," please end in G major.

Copyright © 1995, AMC Publications
A Division of Alliance Music Publications, Inc.
Houston, Texas
International Copyright Secured   All Rights Reserved

Four Spanish Christmas Carols

Vamos todos a Belén

Traditional Spanish Carol
Arranged by Noe Sanchez

SATB Voices, A cappella

In 2 (♩.=72-76)

Refrano

Va - mos to - dos a Be - lén con a - mor y go - zo;
a - do - re - mos al Se - ñor nues - tro Re - den - tor.

Estrofas

1. De - rra - ma u - na es - tre - lla di - vi - no dul - zor,
2. La no - che fue dí - a un án - gel ba - jó,
3. Fe - li - ces pas - to - res la di - cha tri - un - fó,
4. Fe - li - ces sus - pi - ros mi pe - cho da - rá,

poco rit.   *D.C. al Fine*

her - mo - sa don - ce - lla nos da al Sal - va - dor.
na - dan - do en - tre lu - ces que a - sí nos ha - bló.
el cie - lo se ras - ga la vi - da na - ció.
y ar - dien - te mi len - gua tu a - mor can - ta - rá.

Copyright © 1995, AMC Publications
A Division of Alliance Music Publications, Inc.
Houston, Texas
International Copyright Secured   All Rights Reserved

LESSON 11 — Alleluia

COMPOSER: Will James

CHORAL MUSIC TERMS
- beginning
- dynamic shading
- end
- evaluation
- peak
- phrase
- rhythmic motif

VOICING
SATB

PERFORMANCE STYLE
Moderate
A cappella

FOCUS
- Identify rhythmic motifs.
- Identify and sing musical phrases, using dynamic shading.
- Listen to and evaluate group performance.

Warming Up

Vocal Warm-Up 1
When you take a proper breath, your lungs should expand your waist. Place your hands just above your waist, on your back—thumbs forward. As you inhale, feel your hands separate. As you exhale, feel your hands move back toward each other. Now you know you are breathing properly for singing.

Vocal Warm-Up 2
Sing the exercise below, using the breathing described above. Follow the dynamic markings. Move a half step up on each repeat.

Continue up by half steps.

Loo loo loo loo loo. Loo loo loo loo loo.

Do the same exercise using the following rhythms. How will you change the dynamics? Should you change from *loo*? What will you change to? Why?

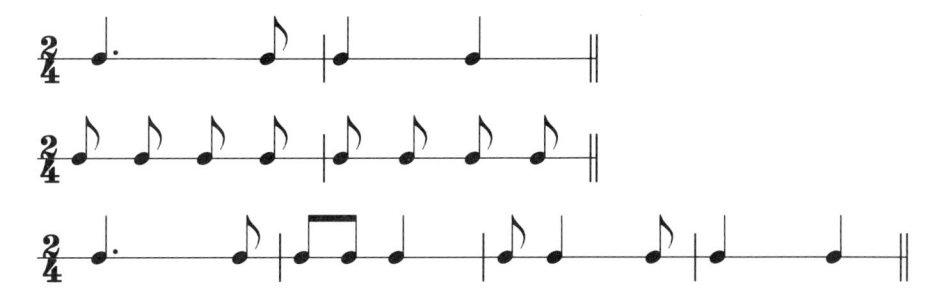

Lesson 11: Alleluia

Sight-Singing

Sight-sing each of the following using solfège and hand signs or numbers. Do you find any rhythm patterns that are repeated? Where do you think the phrases begin, peak, and end? Try them as two-measure, four-measure, and eight-measure phrases, using dynamics to shade them. Which feels the best to you?

Singing: "Alleluia"

Sometimes you hear a short pattern that has meaning, for example:

"Here we go . . ."
". . . gathering at the lake"
" . . . studying for the test"
"Got to stay home . . ."
"I can't believe it . . ."
". . . 99 and 44/100 percent pure"

These catchy little sound bites can be repeated over and over, or combined to create longer ideas. Try each one out, then combine them. (Some combinations make more sense than others.)

A motif is a short musical idea. It can be rhythmic, melodic, or both.

Now turn to the music for "Alleluia" on page 85. Can you find the rhythmic motifs, the patterns that are repeated, in "Alleluia"?

HOW DID YOU DO?

Think about your preparation and performance of "Alleluia."

1. Describe rhythmic motif, then sing a part of this lesson that will demonstrate one.
2. With three classmates, choose a phrase to perform from "Alleluia," then sing it with correct dynamics.
3. What is the difference between a motif and a phrase?
4. How would you assess your ensemble's performance of "Alleluia"? What do you do especially well? What do you need to work on?

84 *Choral Connections Level 3 Mixed Voices*

*To Horatio M. Farrar and the
Southwest Missouri State College Choir, Springfield, MO*

Alleluía

Will James
(ASCAP)

Four-part Chorus SATB A cappella

©Copyright MCMLII by H.T. FitzSimons Company. Renewed 1980. All rights reserved. Made in U.S.A.

Used by Permission.

Alleluia **85**

86 Choral Connections Level 3 Mixed Voices

Alleluia 87

mp
cresc. poco a poco
Al - le - lu - ia, Al - le - lu - ia, Al - le - lu - ia, Al - le-
Al - le - lu - ia, Al - le - lu - ia, Al - le - lu - ia, Al - le-
Al - le - lu - ia, Al - le - lu - ia, Al - le - lu - ia, Al - le-
Al - le - lu - ia, Al - le-
f
lu - ia, Al - le - lu - ia, Al - le - lu - ia, Al - le - lu - ia,
lu - ia, Al - le - lu - ia, Al - le - lu - ia, Al - le - lu - ia,
lu - ia, Al - le - lu - ia, Al - le - lu - ia, Al - le - lu - ia,
lu - ia, Al - le - lu - ia, Al - le - lu - ia, Al - le - lu - ia,

Alleluia

90 Choral Connections Level 3 Mixed Voices

LESSON 12

Flow Gently, Sweet Afton

CHORAL MUSIC TERMS
conducting pattern
legato singing
3/4 meter

Scottish Folk Song
ARRANGER: *John Leavitt*

VOICING
SATB

PERFORMANCE STYLE
Freely
Accompanied

FOCUS
- Read and sing in 3/4 meter.
- Conduct in 3/4 meter.
- Sing, using a legato style.

Warming Up

Vocal Warm-Up

Sing this exercise, moving up by a half step on each repeat. Now try this challenge:
- March in place with light steps on each beat as you sing.
- Add these arm movements: fists down on beat 1, chest level on beat 2, straight overhead on 3, back to chest on 4. How well coordinated are you?

Hoo hoo hoo hoo hoo hoo hoo hoo hoo hoo hoo hoo hoo.

Continue up by half steps.

If you were going to sing this exercise in a legato style, what would you need to change? Give it a try!

Sight-Singing

Sight-sing each part on solfège and hand signs or numbers, using legato articulation. Combine the parts in different ways. Create an arrangement using unison and combination singing of the parts.

so
5

Lesson 12: *Flow Gently, Sweet Afton*

Singing: "Flow Gently, Sweet Afton"

Trace the shape of a large wheel in front of you with both hands, fingers relaxed and palms down. You are making the shape of a circle in the air. Now add weight at the bottom of the circle. Feel the weight at the bottom, and the release on the movement up and around.

In 3/4 meter, the first beat of each measure has the weight, and beats 2 and 3 receive less stress. Try conducting in 3/4 meter.

· Following the diagram at the right, conduct in 3/4 as you listen to "Flow Gently, Sweet Afton."

Now turn to the music for "Flow Gently, Sweet Afton" on page 93.

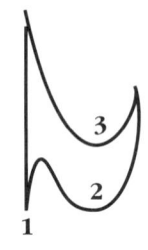

HOW DID YOU DO?

A peaceful song can be a source of inspiration and learning. Think about your preparation and performance of "Flow Gently, Sweet Afton."

1. Sing "Flow Gently, Sweet Afton," conducting in 3/4 meter.
2. Choose a phrase to sing that will demonstrate your ability to sing in legato style.
3. What is the message of "Flow Gently, Sweet Afton"? Do you know any other songs that communicate this mood or message? Would you consider this a good song? Why or why not?

92   *Choral Connections   Level 3 Mixed Voices*

For the Schuykill Chorale, Penn State University, Tom Anderson, Director

Flow Gently, Sweet Afton

Scottish Folk Song
Setting by John Leavitt

SATB, Accompanied

Freely (♩ = ca. 84)

Piano

simile

gent-ly sweet__ Af - ton a - mong thy green__ braes,__ 1. flow
3. flow

Oo

Copyright © 1988 by STUDIO 224, c/o CPP/Belwin, Inc., Miami, FL 33014
International Copyright Secured   Made in U.S.A.   All Rights Reserved

94 Choral Connections Level 3 Mixed Voices

* Although the optional accompaniment is provided here, it is preferred that this section be a cappella.

Flow Gently, Sweet Afton

34
35
36
37
wood - lands the primroses - es blow; there oft, as mild
38
39
40
41
ev'n - ing weeps o - ver the lea, the sweet scent - ed
42
43
44
45
birk shades my Ma - ry and me.
mp
simile

Flow Gently, Sweet Afton 97

LESSON 13

Jesu Dulcis Memoria

COMPOSER: *Tomás Luis de Victoria (c. 1548–1611)*

CHORAL MUSIC TERMS
major
minor
text
tonality
tone color

VOICING
SATB

PERFORMANCE STYLE
Slowly
A cappella

FOCUS
- Read and sing in C major and C minor.
- Explore the relationship between text, tonality, and tone color to create mood.

Warming Up

Vocal Warm-Up

Sing this exercise using solfège and hand signs or numbers. Notice the different tonalities. Do they evoke different moods? How are A, B, and C different?

Try singing in these vocal tone colors: bright, dull, hazy, glaring, hot, cool, muted, foggy (think of some more by yourself). Let your body respond naturally to the tone color you sing, showing the mood through your posture and expression. You might choose consonant/vowel combinations that fit the mood you are singing, for example: *bah* for dull, and *doot* for bright.

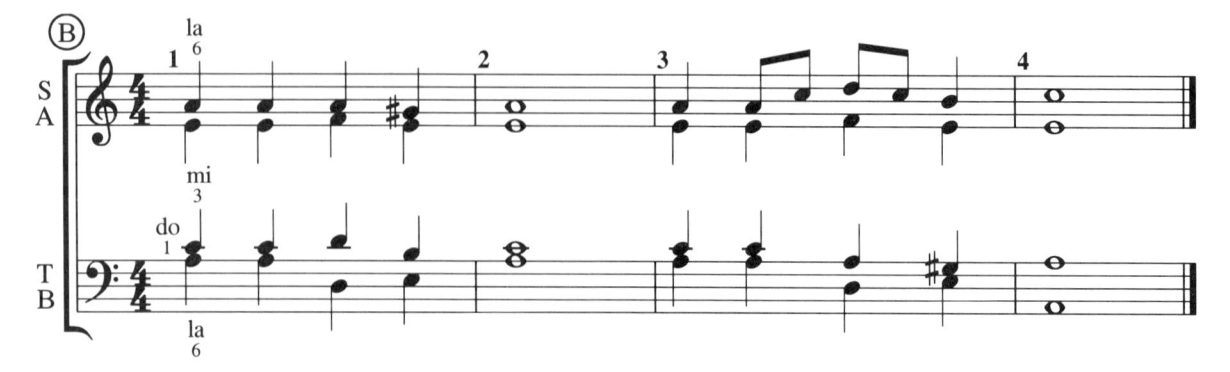

98 *Choral Connections   Level 3 Mixed Voices*

Sight-Singing

Sight-sing this melody using solfège and hand signs or numbers.

Singing: "Jesu Dulcis Memoria"

The mood of a song is communicated through many elements. Three of these are tonality, text, and tone color.

- *Tonality* is the key in which the music is written. Most Western art music is written in major or minor tonalities.
- *Text* is the words, usually set in a poetic style to express a central thought, idea, moral, or narrative.
- *Tone color* is the unique quality of sound produced by a voice or an instrument.

Read the text of "Jesu Dulcis Memoria," and tell what tonality and tone color you would choose if you were going to write a musical setting.

Now turn to the music for "Jesu Dulcis Memoria" on page 100.

HOW DID YOU DO?

What mood expresses your opinion about your own learning in this lesson? Think about your preparation and performance of "Jesu Dulcis Memoria."

1. What three elements did you explore in this lesson that contribute to mood? Describe each in one sentence.

2. Tell what choices the composer made about these three elements. What choices did you make as a performing group? What mood were you trying to convey, and how effective would this combination be for an audience?

3. In a small group, sing a segment of this lesson to illustrate your understanding of the relationship of these three elements.

Jesu Dulcis Memoria

Phonetic Text

Ee-yeh-soo dool-chees meh-maw-ree-ah,
Dahns veh-ra cawr-dee gah-oo-dee-ah gah-oo-dee-ah;
Sehd soo-pehr mehl eht awm-nee-ah,
Eh-ee-yoos dool-chees preh-sehn-tsee-ah.

Tomás Luis de Victoria
Edited by Dean Davids

SATB Mixed Chorus

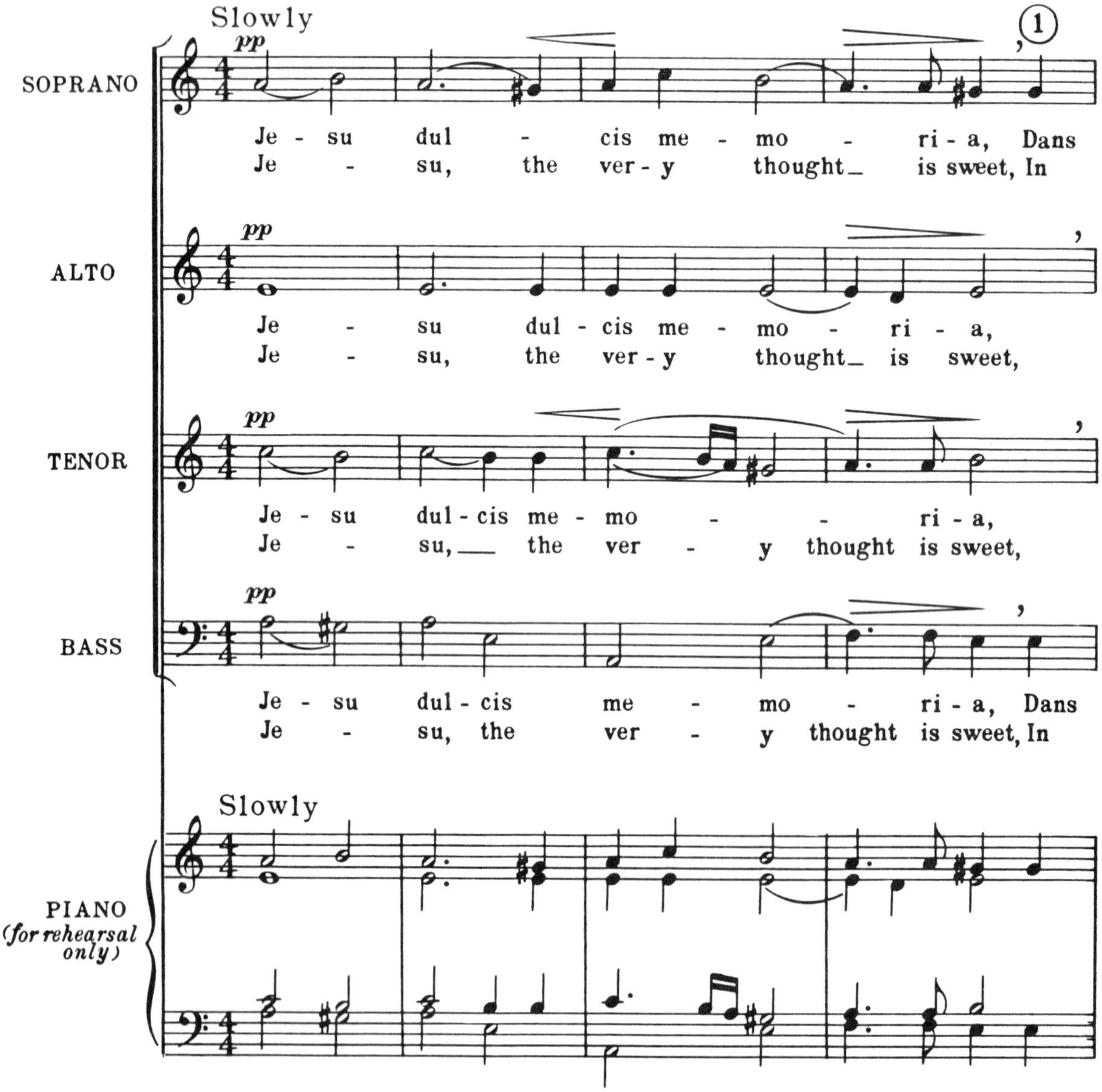
Slowly
SOPRANO
Je - su dul - cis me - mo - ri - a, Dans
Je - su, the ver - y thought_ is sweet, In
ALTO
Je - su dul - cis me - mo - ri - a,
Je - su, the ver - y thought_ is sweet,
TENOR
Je - su dul - cis me - mo - ri - a,
Je - su,_ the ver - y thought is sweet,
BASS
Je - su dul - cis me - mo - ri - a, Dans
Je - su, the ver - y thought is sweet, In
Slowly
PIANO (for rehearsal only)

Copyright 1959 by BELWIN, Inc.
International Copyright Secured
c/o CPP/BELWIN, INC., Miami, Florida 33014

Jesu Dulcis Memoria

2
a tempo mf
- di - a; Sed su-per mel et o - -
- joys meet; But sweet-er than the hon - -
mf
- di - a; Sed su - per mel et o - -
- joys meet; But sweet - er than the hon - -
mf
gau - di - a; Sed su - per mel et o - -
- joys meet; But sweet - er than the hon - -
mf
p
- di - a, Sed su - per mel et o - mni - -
- joys meet; But sweet-er than the hon - ey
a tempo
- mni - a, su - per mel et o - mni -
- ey far, sweet - er than the hon - ey
- mni - a, su - per mel et o - mni -
- ey far, sweet - er than the hon - ey
- mni - a, su - per mel et o - mni -
- ey far, sweet - er than the hon - ey
a, et o - mni -
far, but sweet - er

Jesu Dulcis Memoria

LESSON 14

May the Road Rise to Meet You

CHORAL MUSIC TERMS
ascending intervals
chord progression
legato style

Irish Blessing
COMPOSER: *David Hamilton*

VOICING
SATB

PERFORMANCE STYLE
Slowly, legato
Accompanied by organ (or piano may be substituted)

FOCUS
- Read and sing ascending melodic skips.
- Sing in legato style.

Warming Up

Vocal Warm-Up
Sing these two four-part exercises. As you end each chord progression, move up by a half step. Pay sharp attention to tuning and legato style, and challenge yourself to see how accurately you can tune with the ensemble.

Sight-Singing
Sight-sing the folk song-like exercise on page 105 using solfège and hand signs or numbers. Move from chord to chord carefully, tuning each pitch. Then sing on *loo*, shaping the phrases, with legato style. Notice the ascending skips of more than a third, and practice them carefully.

104 *Choral Connections Level 3 Mixed Voices*

Singing: "May the Road Rise to Meet You"

Sometimes music is used to enhance an already powerful message. Read this Irish Blessing aloud.

> May the road rise to meet you. May the wind be always at your back,
> the sun shine warm upon your face, the rain fall soft upon your fields,
> and until we meet again, may God hold you in His hand,
> may God hold you in the hollow of His hand. Amen.

How are the images in the poem related to real-life situations? What musical elements would you use to enhance this message?

Now turn to the music for "May the Road Rise to Meet You" on page 106.

HOW DID YOU DO?

Did the images in the poem help you learn this piece? Think about your preparation and performance of "May the Road Rise to Meet You."

1. What was easy for you in learning this piece? What was a challenge?

2. Describe an ascending melodic skip, and tell which skips are difficult for you. Choose a phrase of the piece to sing that was a challenge you overcame.

3. Why is legato style appropriate for this piece? Choose three classmates and sing a phrase, demonstrating it with and without legato style singing.

4. Do you think the composer enhanced the text with his music? Give specific musical examples to support your answer.

Lesson 14: *May the Road Rise to Meet You*

May the Road Rise to Meet You

Irish Blessing
Music by David Hamilton

SATB, with Organ Accompaniment

May the Road Rise to Meet You

108 *Choral Connections   Level 3 Mixed Voices*

May the Road Rise to Meet You

ritard
a tempo
cresc.
of His hand, A - men, A -
of His hand, A - men, A -
of His hand, A - men, A -
of His hand, A - men, A -
p
ritard
a tempo
cresc.
ritard
pp
- men, A - men.
men, A - men, A - men.
- men, A - men.
- men, A - men.
pp
ritard

LESSON 15

In Memoria Aeterna

Psalm 112
COMPOSER: Antonio Vivaldi (1678–1741)
ENGLISH TEXT: Douglas R. McEwen

CHORAL MUSIC TERMS
fugue
round

VOICING
SATB

PERFORMANCE STYLE
Andante molto
Accompanied by keyboard

FOCUS
- Identify round and fugal form.
- Distinguish between round and fugal form.
- Sing in fugal form.

Warming Up

Vocal Warm-Up

Sing this warm-up exercise with a lot of energy. Repeat moving up or down by half steps. Bend from the waist and touch your toes on the top pitch on each repetition—and don't bend your knees! Stretch and strengthen your range.

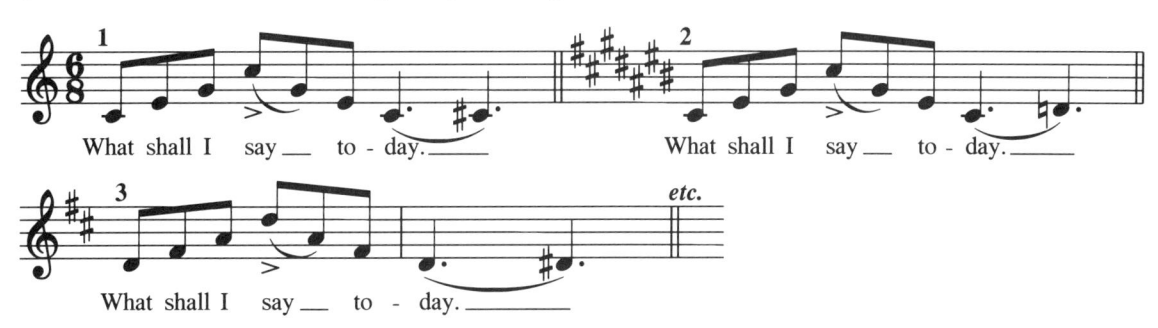

Sight-Singing

Sight-sing this exercise using solfège and hand signs or numbers. Divide into two groups, then sing it as a round, with group II beginning in measure 2.

Singing: "In Memoria Aeterna"

You know how to sing a round, but do you know the difference between a round and a fugue? Sing some rounds you know, then create a definition of round. A fugue is similar to a round, but there are some important differences. Like a round, a fugue is based on the principle of imitation. What else might be different?

Now turn to the music for "In Memoria Aeterna" on page 113.

HOW DID YOU DO?

Think about your preparation and performance of "In Memoria Aeterna."

1. Describe a round and a fugue, and the differences and similarities. Is it easier to sing a round or a fugue? Is it more enjoyable to sing a round or a fugue?

2. In a group, find a way to demonstrate a round and a fugue, using materials from this lesson.

3. How would you rate the ensemble's performance of "In Memoria Aeterna"? What criteria will you use other than the ability to correctly perform the fugue form? What was the most challenging aspect for you? What was the most challenging aspect for the group?

In Memoria Aeterna

(For the Righteous Shall be Remembered)

Mixed Voices* SATB, Accompanied

Antonio Vivaldi (1678–1741)
Edited by Douglas R. McEwen
Psalm 112 from *Beatus* Vir
English text by Douglas R. McEwen

*Altos and Sopranos may sing if a soft balance can be maintained.
**Softly "floated" tone should be sung clearly and actively.

Copyright © 1976 by Hinshaw Music, Inc.
P. O. Box 470 Chapel Hill, N. C. 27514
Reprinted by Permission.

In Memoria Aeterna 113

20
ter-na e - rit jus - tus, in me-mo-ri-a ae-
ev-er be re-mem - bered, for the right-eous shall for-
[p dolce]
In me - mo - ri-a ae-ter - na, ae-ter-na e -
For the right - eous shall for-ev - er, for-ev-er be
[p dolce]
In me -
For the
24
ter - na e-rit ju - stus, e-rit ju - stus, in me-mo - ri-a ae-
ev - er be re-mem - bered, be re-mem - bered, for the right - eous shall for-
rit ju - stus, e-rit ju - stus, in me-mo - ri-a ae-
re-mem - bered, be re-mem - bered, for the right - eous shall for-
mo - ri- a ae - ter - na, ae-ter-na e - - rit ju -
right - eous shall for - ev - er, for-ev-er be re-mem -

In Memoria Aeterna

36

– rit ju – stus: non
re – mem – bered. He
– rit ju – stus: ab au - di- ti- o-ne
re–mem – bered. He shall fear no e–vil
rit ju – stus:
re – mem – bered.
tr.

40

ti – – me – – – – – bit,
shall fear not,
ma-la non ti - me-bit, non ti - me-bit, non ti - me bit, non
tid-ings, e – vil tid-ings, e – vil tid-ings, e – vil tid-ings, he
ab au - di- ti- o-ne
He shall fear no e–vil

In Memoria Aeterna

52
me - - bit, non ti - me - bit, ab au- di-ti-o-ne
tid - - ings, e - vil tid - ings, he shall fear no e-vil
- bit, non ti- me - - bit, non ti - me-bit, non
- ings, e - vil tid - - ings, e - vil tid-ings, he
- bit, non ti - me - bit, non ti - me-bit,
- ings, e - vil tid - ings, e - vil tid-ings,
56
ma la non ti - me-bit, non ti - me-bit, non ti - me-bit,
tid-ings, e - vil tid-ings, e - vil tid-ings, e - vil tid-ings,
ti - - me - - - bit, ab au- di-ti-o-ne
shall fear not he shall fear no e-vil
non
he

In Memoria Aeterna

120 Choral Connections Level 3 Mixed Voices

In Memoria Aeterna

Making Historical Connections

The Adoration of the Magi by Sandro Botticelli (1445–1510) reflects the Renaissance interest in religious subjects. Framing the central figures within the strong geometric pillars emphasized those subjects over others. Similar organizational principles are apparent in the Renaissance composers' ability to create intricate polyphonic works.

c. 1481. Sandro Botticelli. *The Adoration of the Magi.* (Detail.) Tempera on wood. 70 x 104 cm (27⅝ x 41″). National Gallery of Art, Washington, D.C. Andrew W. Mellon Collection.

Renaissance Period

c. 1430–1600

After completing this lesson, you will be able to:
- *Describe some of the major developments of the Renaissance period.*
- *Explain the difference between sacred music and secular music.*
- *Discuss the major musical forms of the Renaissance period.*
- *Identify at least three major composers of the Renaissance period.*

In the history of Western Europe, the period from around 1430 until 1600 is called the Renaissance. This name comes from a French word meaning "rebirth," and the period was in many ways a time of rebirth or renewal. The scholars and artists of the Renaissance made a conscious effort to reestablish the standards of intellectual and cultural greatness they saw in the accomplishments of the ancient Greeks and Romans. Although the great figures of the Renaissance may have been looking back to earlier cultures, they were not moving back; instead, they were moving radically ahead into modern times.

A Time of Discovery

The Renaissance was a time of discovery in many fields. Modern science and scientific methods began to develop. Scholars no longer simply accepted what they read. Rather, they realized that careful observation and experimentation could help them draw new conclusions about the world around them. The results of this approach were a series of important advancements in science, mathematics, and technology. Better clocks and navigating instruments became available; scientists began to develop better lenses for instruments such as telescopes and microscopes. Astronomers established that the Earth and other planets revolved around the sun, and the positions of many stars were accurately calculated.

In part because of the technological advances of the period, the Renaissance was an era of increasing exploration and trade. For the first time, European sailing ships reached the southern coast of Africa, the Americas, and India. In 1519, the first successful round-the-world voyage was undertaken. These journeys brought a new, expanding sense of the world and an influx of new ideas—as well as new opportunities for trade—to the people of Renaissance Europe.

One technological advancement of the Renaissance had an impact on many aspects of life: the invention of the printing press with movable type, usually credited to Johann Gutenberg. Until this development, books had been copied by hand. The development of the printing press meant that books could be produced much more quickly and easily, and much less expensively. More and more people had access to books and the ideas they communicated, and thus prepared themselves to take advantage of this opportunity by learning to read both words and music. Books—of facts, of new ideas, and of music—were no longer the property of only the privileged.

COMPOSERS

John Dunstable (c. 1390–1453)
Guillaume Dufay (1400–1474)
Josquin Desprez (c. 1440–1521)
Heinrich Isaac (c. 1450–1517)
Clement Janequin (c. 1485–1560)
Adrian Willaert (1490–1562)
Christopher Tye (c. 1500–c. 1572)
Thomas Tallis (1505–1585)
Andrea Gabrieli (1520–1586)
Giovanni Pierluigi da Palestrina (c. 1525–1594)
Orlande de Lassus (1532–1594)
William Byrd (1543–1623)
Thomas Morley (c. 1557–c. 1603)
Michael Praetorius (c. 1571–1621)
Thomas Weelkes (1575–1623)

ARTISTS

Donatello (1386–1466)
Sandro Botticelli (1445–1510)
Leonardo da Vinci (1452–1519)
Albrecht Dürer (1471–1528)
Michelangelo (1475–1564)
Raphael (1483–1520)
Titian (c. 1488–1576)

AUTHORS

Sir Thomas More (1478–1536)
Martin Luther (1483–1546)
Miguel de Cervantes (1547–1616)
Sir Walter Raleigh (c. 1552–1618)
Sir Philip Sidney (1554–1586)
William Shakespeare (1564–1616)

CHORAL MUSIC TERMS

a cappella
Gregorian chant
madrigal
mass
motet
polyphony
sacred music
secular music

Gutenberg press; beginning of modern printing — c. 1435

Copenhagen becomes Danish capital — 1445

First printed music appears — 1465

1441 — Eton College and King's College, Cambridge, founded

1453 — Ottoman Turks capture Constantinople, marking end of Byzantine Empire

During the Renaissance, the Catholic church gradually lost some of the influence it had exerted as a center of learning, a formidable political power, and an important force in the daily lives of nearly all Europeans. Rejecting the absolute laws set down by the Church, though not necessarily rejecting any faith in God, Renaissance scholars accepted humanism, a belief in the dignity and value of individual human beings. In addition, the first Protestant churches were established, in opposition to the rule of the Catholic hierarchy.

A Renaissance of the Visual Arts

The developments and discoveries of the Renaissance were reflected in the arts of the period. The works of painters and sculptors became more lifelike and realistic. Painters gave new depth to their work by using perspective and by manipulating light and shadow; they also began using oil paints, which allowed them to revise and refine their work. Sculptors created more individualized human figures, and sculpture began to be considered a true art, rather than a craft.

Many paintings and sculptures of the Renaissance depicted religious subjects, especially scenes from the Bible. However, artists increasingly crafted works with non-religious subjects, often taken from Greek and Roman mythology.

Careful observation and an intense interest in the natural world helped Renaissance artists develop more realistic and individualized paintings and sculptures. Some of the most notable artists worked in several media and delved deeply into science as well. Leonardo da Vinci, one of the foremost painters and sculptors of the Renaissance, was also an architect, a scientist, an engineer, and a musician.

The Influence of the Catholic Church on Music

In the centuries preceding the Renaissance—a time usually called the Middle Ages—most composed music was for the Catholic church and performed as part of religious services. The most important musical form of the period was the **Gregorian chant**, *a melody sung in unison by male voices*. The chants were sung **a cappella**, *without instrumental accompaniment*. All the chants were composed in Latin, the language of all Church services at that time, and were based on sacred texts, often from the Book of Psalms in the Old Testament.

Although the earliest Gregorian chants consisted of a single melodic line, a second melodic line was added to most chants during the Middle Ages. This was the beginning of **polyphony**, *the simultaneous performance of two or more melodic lines*. In polyphonic music, each part begins at a different place, and each part is independent and important. The use of various kinds of polyphony has continued through the centuries; in fact, polyphony is a significant feature in some modern jazz compositions.

126 *Choral Connections Level 3 Mixed Voices*

da Vinci sketches an early helicopter design | 1483

Columbus lands in West Indies/Americas | 1492

1473-1480 Sistine Chapel built

1488 Diaz sails around the Cape of Good Hope

1498 da Gama sails around Africa and lands in India

The artists and architects of the Renaissance rediscovered Classical antiquity and were inspired by what they found. In 1547, Michelangelo (1475–1564) became chief architect for the replacement of the original basilica of Old St. Peter's. Architect Giacomo della Porta finished the dome 26 years after Michelangelo's death.

1546–64. Michelangelo. Exterior view, St. Peter's. St. Peter's Basilica, Vatican State, Rome, Italy. (Dome completed by Giacomo della Porta, 1590.)

Sacred Music of the Renaissance

During the Renaissance, the Catholic church continued to exert a strong influence on daily life and on the arts. Much of the important music composed during the Renaissance was **sacred music**, *music used in religious services.*

The two most important forms of sacred Renaissance music were the **mass**—*a long musical composition that includes the five major sections of the Catholic worship service*—and the **motet**—*a shorter choral work, set to Latin texts and used in religious services, but not part of the regular mass.* In the early years of the Renaissance, one of the most influential composers

1508 Sistine Chapel ceiling painted by Michelangelo

1517 Protestant Reformation begins in Germany with Luther's 95 Theses

1519 Cortez conquers Mexico

1519 Magellan begins voyage around the world

1529 Women seen for the first time on Italian stages

1531 Henry VIII declared head of the Church of England

1545 Council of Trent meets to discuss Reformation and Counter Reformation

of both masses and motets was John Dunstable. Dunstable developed a new harmonic structure of polyphony; his music helped establish the Renaissance as the "golden age of polyphony."

Later in the period, Josquin Desprez began to change the sound of Renaissance choral music. He believed that music should be structured to make the words of the text understandable, and he also thought that all the voices in a choral setting could be equal in importance. Desprez is considered one of the founders of Renaissance music, because he introduced three new musical concepts:

1. Homophonic harmonies, produced by chords that support a melody;
2. Motive imitation, short repeating melodies between voice parts;
3. A more natural cadence, or sense of conclusion.

During the Renaissance, instruments were added to accompany and echo the voices used in sacred music. Adrian Willaert was one of the first composers to combine voices, pipe organs, and other instruments. He also began to use dynamics and was among the first to compose for two imitative voices.

The first music for Protestant religious services was written during this period. Here, sacred music was sung not in Latin but in the languages of the worshipers. One of the most important leaders of the Protestant Reformation, Martin Luther, wrote German hymns that are still sung in Protestant churches today.

The Evolution of Secular Music

Secular music, *any music that is not sacred*, changed in quality and quantity during the Renaissance period. Secular music became increasingly important as the center of musical activity began to shift from churches to castles and towns. Many court and town musicians traveled throughout Europe, so new styles and musical ideas spread relatively rapidly.

The **madrigal**, *a secular form of music written in several imitative parts*, became popular during the Renaissance. Madrigals were composed by such musicians as Clement Janequin, Heinrich Isaac, Thomas Tallis, William Byrd, Thomas Morley, and Thomas Weelkes, to be sung by everyday people. Whole collections of songs in the madrigal form were printed in part books. A family might purchase a set of part books (one for soprano, one for alto, and so on); then family members and friends would gather around these part books and sing.

Most madrigals were composed for three or more voices. Typically, a madrigal was based on a secular poem and incorporated the expression of strong emotions, usually about love. The polyphony within madrigals was often quite challenging, even though the songs were intended primarily for home entertainment. Europeans of the noble and emerging middle classes placed an increased importance on the education of the individual; reading music and singing were considered essential aspects of that education.

1558	1574	c. 1590
Elizabeth I crowned Queen of England (died 1603)	Portuguese colonize Angola and found São Paulo	William Shakespeare begins play writing

1564	1584	1599
First violins made by Andrea Amati	Sir Walter Raleigh discovers Virginia	Globe Theatre built in London

Check Your Understanding

Recall

1. What were the most important differences between the music of the Middle Ages and the music of the Renaissance?
2. What is a cappella music?
3. What is polyphony?
4. What is the difference between a mass and a motet?
5. What is the difference between sacred music and secular music?
6. How are motets and madrigals alike? How are they different?

Thinking It Through

1. The word *polyphony* comes from two roots: poly, meaning *many*, and phony, meaning *sounds*. Explain the relationship between these roots and polyphonic music.
2. If you listened to a piece of unidentified music, what clues could help you decide whether it was a Renaissance composition?

RENAISSANCE CONNECTIONS

Listening to...
Renaissance Music

CHORAL SELECTION

Thomas Weelkes — "As Vesta Was Descending"

Thomas Weelkes (1575–1623), an organist and church composer, was one of England's best madrigalists. "As Vesta Was Descending" is in a collection of madrigals called *The Triumphes of Oriana*, published in 1601. This is a six-voice madrigal that uses text painting.

In the song "As Vesta Was Descending," Vesta is portrayed as the Roman goddess of the hearth fire coming down the hill with her servants, "Diana's darlings." (Diana is the protector of servants.) At the same time, Oriana (Queen Elizabeth I) is climbing the hill with her shepherd followers. When Vesta's attendants see the Queen, they desert Vesta and hurry down the hill to join Oriana, whereupon everyone sings the Queen's praises.

INSTRUMENTAL SELECTION

Andrea Gabrieli — Ricercar in the Twelfth Mode

Andrea Gabrieli (1520–1586) was the organist at St. Mark's Cathedral in Venice, Italy, from 1564 until his death. He composed instrumental as well as sacred and secular vocal music.

A *ricercar* is a polyphonic instrumental composition that uses imitation. "In the Twelfth Mode" means that it is based on a scale corresponding to C major.

RENAISSANCE CONNECTIONS

Introducing...
"O Domine Jesu Christe"

Giovanni Pierluigi da Palestrina

Setting the Stage

As you sing "O Domine Jesu Christe," you will perform the musical elements of which you have read: the feeling of central key (tonality) and the flow of the individual part lines resulting in chords (harmony), which are very pleasant to hear. Listen carefully for the interplay of rhythm between two parts as the piece is performed (for example, in measures 5 and 6, between the alto, tenor, and bass lines). Palestrina's techniques of composition lived long after his death, forming a solid basis for the music of the future beyond the Renaissance period. You can appreciate his contributions to our music today because most of our songs are written in major or minor keys. This musical theory was one that Palestrina helped solidify.

Meeting the Composer
Giovanni Pierluigi da Palestrina (c. 1525–1594)

Giovanni Pierluigi da Palestrina is considered to be the master of Renaissance church music. He refined the motet and the mass partly in an effort to honor the Roman Catholic Church's request that music consider the text as the primary factor of composition, keeping the music objective, rational, logical, emotionally restrained, balanced, and ordered. As one sings Palestrina's music, the linear motion of and logical voice leadings in each part line results in harmonies that are recognizable and pleasing to our "modern" ears.

RENAISSANCE LESSON

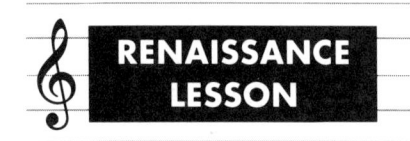

O Domine Jesu Christe

Latin Text
COMPOSER: *Giovanni Pierluigi da Palestrina* (c. 1525–1594)
ARRANGER: *Gerald Knight*

CHORAL MUSIC TERMS
a cappella
homophonic
imitation
polyphonic
Renaissance

VOICING
SATB

PERFORMANCE STYLE
Andante
A cappella

FOCUS
- Visually and aurally identify homophonic texture.
- Sing homophonic texture.
- Sing a Renaissance piece a cappella.

Warming Up

Vocal Warm-Up
Sing the following exercise using solfège and hand signs or numbers, then on *loo*. Move down by a half step on each repeat. Is this an example of *homophonic* or *polyphonic* texture? How do you know?

Sight-Singing
Sight-sing this exercise using solfège and hand signs or numbers. Although this is written in homophonic style, there are a few interesting places where voices move independently. Watch and listen carefully, tuning your own voice part to those around you. When you sing with no accompaniment, it is called *a cappella*.

132 *Choral Connections Level 3 Mixed Voices*

Singing: "O Domine Jesu Christe"

Imagine that you have a set of square blocks on a desk. How would you arrange them so they represented polyphony, several voice parts supporting each other but moving independently?

How would you arrange them differently to represent homophony, several voice parts moving together in block chords?

Now turn to the music for "O Domine Jesu Christe" on page 134.

HOW DID YOU DO?

Just like block chords have pitches supporting one another, your ensemble provides support for you as a singer.

Think about your preparation and performance of "O Domine Jesu Christe."

1. Describe the difference between polyphony and homophony, and apply these descriptions to "O Domine Jesu Christe."

2. How can you identify homophony visually? aurally?

3. How can you tell that this is a Renaissance period piece? What clues can be found in the notation? What clues can be found in the sound?

O Domine Jesu Christe **133**

O Domine Jesu Christe

(O Lord Jesus Christ)

Giovanni Pierluigi da Palestrina (c. 1525–1594)
Edited and Arranged by Gerald Knight
(English text by Gerald Knight)
(ASCAP)

A cappella Chorus of Mixed Voices

Copyright © MCMLXVII by Carl Fischer, Inc., New York
International Copyright Secured
Copying or reproducing this publication in whole or in part
violates the Federal Copyright Law.
All rights reserved including public performance for profit.

Duration
1 min. 15 sec.

134 *Choral Connections Level 3 Mixed Voices*

O Domine Jesu Christe

136 *Choral Connections Level 3 Mixed Voices*

▲ **Attention to detail, particularly in direct and reflected light in mirrors and doorways, characterizes this work of Diego Velázquez (1599–1660). The challenge to the viewer to find all the images in *Las Meninas* equals the challenge to comprehend the intricacies in a Bach fugue or concerto, representative musical works of the same period.**

1656. Diego Velázquez. *Las Meninas*. Oil on canvas. 3.20 x 2.76 m (10'5" x 9'). Museo del Prado, Madrid, Spain.

Baroque Period

1600–1750

After completing this lesson, you will be able to:
- Describe the general characteristics of Baroque visual arts.
- Discuss the most important differences between Renaissance music and Baroque music.
- Identify at least five new musical forms of the Baroque period.
- Identify at least four major composers of the Baroque period.

The artworks of the Renaissance reflect the ideas and ideals of the period. They are balanced and restrained; they communicate a sense of calm. The next period of European history—the Baroque period, which lasted from about 1600 until around 1750—was an age of reaction against the restraint and balance of the Renaissance. Baroque artists expressed the ideals of their own time by adding emotion, decoration, and opulence to their works.

A Time of Continued Development

The explorations and developments of the Renaissance continued into the Baroque period. European trade with distant lands increased, and European kingdoms sought to expand their power by establishing empires. The first European settlers left their homes and sailed to the Americas. People had a growing sense of possibility and excitement.

The study of science and mathematics continued to advance, and new technological developments were made. The basis of modern chemistry was established, and medical research, as well as medical practices, improved. The study of science became a more complex and consuming endeavor, one that no longer attracted the special interests of artists.

During the Baroque period, aristocrats—including emperors, kings, princes, and other nobles—seemed intent on displaying their wealth and power. Part of this display involved attracting great artists, including musicians, to their courts. Both the aristocracy and the Catholic church were generous patrons of the arts throughout the Baroque period. The artworks created during the Baroque period are typically large in scale and dramatic in effect. Painters and sculptors of the time built upon the forms established by Renaissance artists and added their own complex details and dramatic elaborations.

Baroque Music

Baroque music reflected the same style exhibited in the visual arts of the time; it was written on a grand scale, full of vitality and emotion. Compositions typically had a strong sense of movement, often including a **continuo**, *a continually moving bass line.* Usually the melody was highly ornamental. In many compositions, additional ornamentations were improvised, or invented on the spur of the moment during performances.

COMPOSERS
Claudio Monteverdi (1567–1643)
Arcangelo Corelli (1643–1713)
Henry Purcell (1659–1695)
Antonio Vivaldi (1678–1741)
Georg Philipp Telemann (1681–1767)
Johann Sebastian Bach (1685–1750)
George Frideric Handel (1685–1759)

ARTISTS
El Greco (1541–1614)
Michelangelo da Caravaggio (c. 1565–1609)
Peter Paul Rubens (1577–1640)
Frans Hals (1580–1666)
Artemisia Gentileschi (1593–1653)
Gianlorenzo Bernini (1598–1680)
Diego Velázquez (1599–1660)
Rembrandt van Rijn (1606–1669)
Judith Leyser (1609–1660)

AUTHORS
John Donne (c. 1573–1631)
Rene Descartes (1596–1650)
John Milton (1608–1674)
Molière (1622–1673)

CHORAL MUSIC TERMS
arias
cantata
chorale
concerto grosso
continuo
movements
opera
oratorio
recitative
suite

Galileo	Henry Hudson explores the Hudson River	Pilgrims land in America		Isaac Newton	Quakers arrive in Massachusetts
1564–1642	1609	1620		1642–1727	1656

1607	1618–1648	1636	1643–1715
Jamestown, Virginia, established settlement	Thirty Years' War	Harvard College founded	Reign of Louis XIV as King of France

1608
Telescope invented in Holland

During this period, instrumental music gained in importance, both in the church and as music commissioned for the entertainment of the courts of Europe. Vocal music also underwent changes. Instrumental accompaniments were increasingly added to both sacred and secular vocal works, and several new musical forms developed.

Instrumental Forms

As instrumental music grew more important, the musical instruments themselves were refined and their uses changed. The violin, previously a solo instrument, was added to ensemble groups. The harpsichord and the organ became the most important keyboard instruments.

Longer instrumental works were composed during the Baroque period. Often, these compositions consisted of several **movements**, *individual pieces that sound fairly complete within themselves but are part of a longer work.*

One of the new instrumental forms of the Baroque period was the **concerto grosso**. This *composition for a small chamber orchestra consists of several movements and features a moving bass line and an elaborate melody.* Most of the major Baroque composers wrote concerti grossi. Among the best known are *The Four Seasons* by Antonio Vivaldi and the set of six *Brandenburg Concertos* by Johann Sebastian Bach.

Another instrumental form that developed was the **suite**, *a set of musical movements, usually inspired by dances, of contrasting tempos and styles.* Suites and suite-related compositions were very popular during this time; the most famous suites were those composed by Bach.

▲ **The ornate interior decor is reflected endlessly in the Hall of Mirrors, designed by François de Cuvilliés (1696–1768). Musical embellishment and ornamentation of the Baroque period provide similar stylistic elements in compositions by Johann Sebastian Bach and his contemporaries.**

1734–39. François de Cuvilliés. Hall of Mirrors, Amalienburg, Munich, Germany.

Vocal and Mixed Forms

Vocal music became more varied and notably more dramatic during the Baroque period. Sacred music continued to be predominantly choral, but new instrumental accompaniment added greater variety and strength to many compositions. One of the new forms of the Baroque period was the **chorale**, or *hymn tune.* Chorales were

Timeline

- **1682** — LaSalle explores the Mississippi
- **1685–1750** — Johann Sebastian Bach
- **1685–1759** — George Frideric Handel
- **1687** — Publication of Newton's *Mathematical Principles*
- **1704** — First American newspaper established, *Boston News Letter*
- **1706–1790** — Benjamin Franklin
- **1710** — Handel comes to England

---

composed for Lutheran services, using German texts. They were easy to sing and to remember, so all members of a church congregation could join in.

A related Baroque form was the **cantata**, *a collection of compositions with instrumental accompaniment consisting of several movements based on related secular or sacred text segments.* The fact that this form could be composed as either a sacred or a secular work itself marks a new development of the period. Music directors at important Protestant churches were required to compose cantatas for weekly services. Bach, who served as a music director in Leipzig for 25 years, composed nearly 300 sacred cantatas.

Another mixed form from the Baroque period is the **oratorio**, *a composition for solo voices, chorus, and orchestra, that was an extended dramatic work on a literary or religious theme presented without theatrical action.* Like a cantata, an oratorio was composed to be performed in a concert setting, without costumes and scenery. However, the oratorio was written on a larger scale and told a story, usually religious, with plot and resolution. The oratorio was typically performed by a small chorus, an orchestra, and four vocal soloists.

Of all the new musical forms that developed during the Baroque period, perhaps the most characteristic is the **opera**, *a combination of singing, instrumental music, dancing, and drama that tells a story.* Opera combined many art forms, including drama, dance, architecture, and visual art, with music. And, in the true sense of Baroque style, opera was emotional and lavish. The best known composers of Baroque opera were Claudio Monteverdi, who wrote *Orfeo*, the first important opera, in 1607, and Henry Purcell.

The highlights of most operas are the **arias**, *dramatic songs for solo voices with orchestral accompaniment.* Another important feature of an opera is the **recitative**, *a vocal line that imitates the rhythm of speech.*

Check Your Understanding

Recall

1. What is a continuo?
2. What is a concerto grosso? Which Baroque composers are particularly remembered for this kind of composition?
3. What is a cantata?
4. What is the difference between an oratorio and an opera?
5. How are an aria and a recitative alike? How are they different?
6. List at least three adjectives you would use to describe the music of the Baroque period.

Thinking It Through

1. Identify one Baroque composition you have listened to. What characteristics mark that composition as a Baroque work?
2. For whom was Baroque music written? Who were the intended performers and the intended audience?

BAROQUE CONNECTIONS

Listening to...

Baroque Music

CHORAL SELECTION

Handel — *Messiah*, "Hallelujah" Chorus

George Frideric Handel (1685–1759) was a contemporary of Johann Sebastian Bach. Handel's compositions, great in number, were mostly English oratorios and Italian operas. Of all of his works, *Messiah* is the most well known. It is also exceptional in that it has no plot and is based on Old and New Testament passages of the Bible. *Messiah* was written in less than a month and was first performed in Ireland in 1741. It did not gain favor in England until a decade after its first performance in 1742. However, since that time it has grown to have tremendous popularity, being one of the favorite musical works of the Christmas and Easter holiday seasons.

INSTRUMENTAL SELECTION

Bach — Organ Fugue in G Minor (*Little Fugue*)

Johann Sebastian Bach (1685–1750) was born into a family of musicians. Through his lifetime, he held many positions as organist and church musician, the longest standing being at Weimar, Cothen, and Leipzig. During his employment at Cothen, Bach composed mostly secular works (at the request of the prince, his benefactor). For nearly all of his career as a composer he wrote music for the organ. His organ music has a characteristic use of the obbligato pedals, contributing yet again to the elaborate style that we associate with music from the Baroque period.

THE BRAIN-SAVING DIET? THINK FRUITS AND NUTS

By JEFF NESMITH
hjnesmith@ajc.com

Washington — Some scientists are beginning to think that eating certain fruits and nuts may delay old-age problems like Alzheimer's disease.

Blueberries, apples, blackberries, strawberries, spinach, walnuts and that old retirement community standby, prunes, are seen as promising candidates.

Studies on rats and mice show the theory holds promise, according to James Joseph, a U.S. Department of Agriculture researcher. He is a leading proponent of the idea that some foods inhibit inflammation or contain antioxidants that counter the buildup of destructive "free radicals" — highly reactive atoms or molecules that attack disease-causing organisms but also can damage human cells.

But there's no breakthrough dis-

➤ Please see **BRAIN, A12**

When you pair the two-mode tech
Tahoe Hybrid gets up to 40% better city fu
hardworking hybrid. And joining our Tahoe Hy
Do more. Use less. Find out how at chevy.com **AN AME**

e buyer's
2, should have
the home
s No. 1. The
se the home
ega that had a
ing chair front
e list price was

AIN OPERATOR:
404-526-5151

The Atlanta Journal-Constitution
ajc.com

0-933-9771
are

-impaired) for
elivery, classified:

condition and in the
days. If an error occurs
s, before 1 p.m. on

f town, report a service

y the convenience of

Holiday and bonus
days include: Jan. 1, Feb.
5, Feb. 19, May 28, July
, Sept. 3, Nov. 22 and
ec. 25. Other bonus
ditions are optional.

etro area. Mail

of the Blind's free
1-888-882-1629.

rnal (est. 1883) and
y day of the year.
ostage paid at Atlanta,
higher in outlying areas.
Circulation, P.O. Box

2007 Chevy Tahoe LTZ shown. *Based on 2007 GM segmentation and 2008 EPA estimates. Tahoe 2WD with available 5
14 city/20 hwy. †Limited availability in select markets starting fall 2007. See chevy.com/hybrid for details. ** Tahoe Hybri
Based on GM testing. Official EPA estimates not yet available. ©2007 GM Corp. Buckle up, America.

BAROQUE CONNECTIONS

Introducing... "Werfet Panier Auf Im Lande"

Georg Philipp Telemann

Setting the Stage

"Werfet Panier Auf Im Lande," attributed to Georg Philipp Telemann, is based on Jeremiah's prophecy in the Bible predicting the destruction of Babylon because of its sinful ways. Keep this theme in mind so that you don't become carried away with the dancelike quality of the music. If Telemann meant for there to be any joy in the music, it is in troops marching to war accompanied by the stirring music of a military band with its trumpet calls.

Meeting the Composer
Georg Philipp Telemann

In his own time, Georg Philipp Telemann (1681–1767) was one of the most highly esteemed of all German musicians. Although he was one of the most prolific composers of all time, he composed in the shadows of Bach and Handel. Perhaps for this reason, this great Baroque composer is hardly more than a name in the twentieth century.

Telemann's vast output of music includes some 40 operas, 700 church cantatas, 44 Passions, 600 French overtures, and innumerable other orchestral, chamber, and harpsichord compositions.

BAROQUE LESSON

Werfet Panier Auf Im Lande

CHORAL MUSIC TERMS
articulation
Baroque
interpretation
mood
motet
6/8 meter

COMPOSER: *Georg Philipp Telemann (1681–1767)*
TEXT: *Jeremiah 51:27–29*

VOICING
SATB

PERFORMANCE STYLE
Rhythmically, like a march
A cappella

FOCUS
- Read and sing in 6/8 meter.
- Interpret a piece to convey a specific mood.

Warming Up

Vocal Warm-Up

Before you begin singing, concentrate on relaxing the jaw and muscles that surround the jaw area, including your neck muscles. Roll your shoulders forward and backward, shake out your arms, move your head/neck area forward, back, and from side to side.

Now, sing this exercise on *mah* or *nah* to develop a resonant tone. Separate the repeated tones for clarity. Move up or down by half steps on each repeat.

Sight-Singing

Before singing this exercise out loud, sing it in your mind. Look at the key signature, meter signature, rhythms, and melodic leaps. Where will you need to really work for accuracy? Now sight-sing this exercise using solfège and hand signs or numbers. What mood does it convey? What can you do to help your singing enhance this mood?

Singing: "Werfet Panier Auf Im Lande"

Music is often played when people gather for special events. Describe the music you would expect to hear at a football game. What kind of music would you expect to hear at a wedding? Describe the music you would expect to hear at a funeral. If selected appropriately, music can enhance the mood of any occasion.

Now turn to the music for "Werfet Panier Auf Im Lande" on page 146.

HOW DID YOU DO?

Think about your preparation and performance of "Werfet Panier Auf Im Lande."
1. Describe how you perform 6/8 meter. Choose a phrase to sing to demonstrate your ability to perform in 6/8 meter.
2. Describe the mood of "Werfet Panier Auf Im Lande," and tell how you performed the music to enhance the mood.
3. Where might you suggest that this piece be performed?
4. Tell why this piece is considered an exemplary model of Baroque vocal music. Give specific musical characteristics.

Werfet Panier Auf Im Lande
(Wave All the Flags in the Country)

Georg Philipp Telemann (1681–1767)
Edited by Abraham Kaplan
Jeremiah 51: 27–29
English version by Joseph Boonin

Motet for Four-part Chorus of Mixed Voices, A cappella

Copyright © 1965 by Tetra Music Corp.

Printed in U.S.A.

146 *Choral Connections Level 3 Mixed Voices*

Werfet Panier Auf Im Lande 147

15
mf cresc.
wer-fet Pa-nier auf im Lan-de. Hei - li-get die Hei - den
wave all the flags in the coun-try. Sanc - ti-fy the na - tions
wer-fet Pa-nier auf im Lan-de. Hei - li-get die
wave all the flags in the coun-try. Sanc - ti-fy the
wer-fet Pa-nier auf im Lan-de. Hei -
wave all the flags in the coun-try. Sanc -
wer-fet Pa-nier auf im Lan-de.
wave all the flags in the coun-try.
S
A
T
B

20
f
mf cresc.
wi - der sie,
though_ they sin,
Hei-li-get die Hei-den wi - der sie,
Sanc-ti-fy e-ven a - gainst_ their will,
Hei - den wi - der sie,
na - tions though_ they sin,
- li-get die Hei - den
- ti-fy the na - tions
Hei - li-get
Sanc - ti-fy
Hei-li-get die Hei-den wi - der sie,
Sanc-ti-fy e-ven a - gainst their will,
S
A
T
B

Werfet Panier Auf Im Lande 149

S
A
T
B
ff
be und er - schre-cke;
ble and be fright-ened;
be - - - - - - - be und er - schre-cke;
trem - - - - - - - ble and be fright-ened;
Land_ er-be - - - - be und er - schre-cke;
land_ shall trem - - - - ble and be fright-ened;
35
mf legato
denn die Ge-dan-ken des Herrn wol-len er-fül - let wer - den
then the com-mand of the Lord shall be per-formed,_ per-formed_ a -
f legato
denn die Ge-dan-ken des Herrn wol-len er-fül - let wer - den
then the com-mand of the Lord shall be per-formed,_ per-formed_ a -
35
mf legato

Werfet Panier Auf Im Lande 151

45
S
nie-mand, da-rin-nen nie-mand, niemand woh - ne,
no one, where dwell-eth no one, no one dwell - eth,
A
nie-mand, da-rin-nen nie - mand, niemand woh-ne, dass er das Land Ba-bel zur
no one, where dwell-eth no one, no one dwell-eth, He will transform Ba-bel in -
T
nie-mand, da-rin-nen nie - mand, niemand woh - ne, dass er das Land
no one, where dwell-eth no one, no one dwell - eth, He will trans-form
B
nie-mand, da-rin-nen nie - mand, niemand woh - ne,
no one, where dwell-eth no one, no one dwell - eth,
45
S
dass er das Land Ba-bel zur Wü - sten ma-che, da -
He will transform Ba-bel in - to a waste-land where
A
Wü - sten ma-che, da - rin - nen nie - mand woh-ne, da - rin - nen
to a waste-land where dwell - eth no one, dwell-eth, where dwell - eth
T
Ba-bel zur Wü - sten ma-che, da-rin-nen nie - mand woh-ne, da -
Ba-bel in-to a wasteland where dwell - eth no one, where dwell-eth
B
dass er das Land Ba-bel zur Wü - sten ma-che, da-rin - nen
He will trans-form Ba-bel in-to a waste-land where dwell - eth

Werfet Panier Auf Im Lande **153**

▲ **Anne Louis Girodet-Trioson, (1767–1824)** through this portrait of *Jean-Baptiste Bellay, Deputy of Santo Domingo*, expressed the interest of Europeans in revolution for the rights of the individual. As visual artists worked with such themes, composers were also influenced by similar revolutionary thought. The *Eroica Symphony in E-Flat* by Beethoven is one of many examples of music inspired by revolution.

1797. Anne Louis Girodet-Trioson. *Jean-Baptiste Bellay, Deputy of Santo Domingo*. Oil on canvas. 160 x 114 cm (63 x 45"). Musée National du Chateau de Versailles, Versailles, France.

Classical Period

1750–1820

After completing this lesson, you will be able to:
- Discuss the major changes that took place during the Classical period.
- Identify the ideals of the Classical arts.
- Discuss the most important musical forms of the Classical period.
- Identify the two most important Classical composers.

COMPOSERS
Franz Joseph Haydn (1732–1809)
Wolfgang Amadeus Mozart (1756–1791)
Luigi Cherubini (1760–1842)
Ludwig van Beethoven (1770–1827)
Vincento Bellini (1801–1835)

ARTISTS
Antoine Watteau (1684–1721)
Francois Boucher (1703–1770)
Jean-Honoré Fragonard (1732–1806)
Francisco Gôya (1746–1828)
Jacques Louis David (1748–1825)
Anne Louis Girodet-Trioson (1767–1824)

AUTHORS
Jonathan Swift (1667–1745)
Samuel Richardson (1689–1761)
Voltaire (1694–1778)
Henry Fielding (1707–1754)
Wolfgang Goethe (1749–1832)
Friedrich von Schiller (1759–1805)
Jane Austen (1775–1817)

The emotion and drama of the Baroque period were followed by the clarity and simplicity of the Classical period. The word *Classical* has many meanings. It refers to the works and ideas of ancient Greece and Rome. It also refers to the period of European art and music that lasted from about 1750 until around 1820. During this time, artists "looked back" to the standards of balance and unity they saw in ancient Greek and Roman artworks.

The Age of Enlightenment

The Classical period is often called the Age of Enlightenment. It was a time when people put their faith in reason and thought, not in tradition and emotion. It was also a time of great faith in "progress." Members of the growing middle classes believed that their rights could and would be established and that the power and privilege of the aristocracy would be curtailed.

The attitudes of the Classical period were reflected in the major political events of the era. The American colonists revolted against their British rulers and established an independent United States. Thirteen years after the signing of the Declaration of Independence, the French Revolution began; this uprising established a new government and a new societal structure in France.

During the Classical period, the Catholic church's support of the arts declined sharply. However, noble and wealthy individuals and families commissioned artworks of all kinds in increasing numbers. In spite of this patronage, some important visual artists created works that poked subtle fun at the activities and attitudes of the aristocracy.

The paintings, sculpture, and architecture of this period are usually referred to as Neoclassical. (The prefix *neo-* adds the meaning "new"; this term distinguishes Neoclassical artworks from the Classical artworks created in ancient Greece and Rome.) Neoclassical works stress the balance and grandeur that artists saw in the ancient Classical works. Painters such as Jacques Louis David used ancient Roman settings and emphasized firm lines and clear structures. The simpler and grand styles developed in painting, sculpture, and architecture were both an evocation of Classical balance and a reaction against the emotional excesses of late Baroque art.

CHORAL MUSIC TERMS
chamber music
sonata form
string quartets
symphony

Swift's *Gulliver's Travels* published
1726

George Washington
1732–1799

Thomas Jefferson
1743–1826

American Revolutionary War fought
1775–1783

1732–1757
Franklin writes *Poor Richard's Almanac*

1775
James Watt invents the steam engine

Music of the Classical Period

Like Neoclassical paintings, sculpture, and architecture, Classical music left behind the extreme drama and emotion of the Baroque period. Exaggerated embellishments and improvisations had no place in Classical compositions. Instead, Classical music emphasized precision and balance. An essential characteristic of the period was a careful balance between the content of the music and the form in which it was expressed.

During this period, middle-class people took an increasing interest in music. Composers responded by writing works that were accessible to the general public. Comic operas began to replace the serious operas of Baroque times. Dance music, including familiar folk tunes, were included in many compositions. Music, like other art forms, gradually became available to a wider range of the population.

Vocal and mixed forms, especially the opera and the oratorio, continued to develop during the Classical period. However, the most important Classical developments came in instrumental music, which gained in importance during this time.

Chamber music—*music for a small group of instruments designed to be played in a room (or chamber) rather than in a public concert hall*—became significant during the Classical period. Such compositions are generally light and entertaining, both for the performers and for the listeners. The most popular Classical chamber music compositions were **string quartets**, *pieces composed for two violins, a viola, and a cello.*

Another important instrumental form of the Classical period was the **sonata form**, *a movement written in A A' B A form*. The sonata form begins with a theme (A), which is then repeated with elaboration (A'). Then comes a contrasting development (B), and the form closes with a return to the original theme (A).

The concerto also changed and developed during the Classical period. The Baroque concerto featured an instrumental group supported by an orchestra. The Classical concerto, by contrast, became a work for an instrumental soloist—often a pianist, but also a violinist, trumpeter, clarinetist, bassoonist, or cellist—and orchestra.

▲ **Interest in archeology, particularly Greek and Roman models, resulted in the design of the library at Kenwood House by Robert Adam. This room combines Roman stucco ornamentation with the symmetry and geometric precision of the Classical period. Symmetry and precision are vital elements in musical compositions of the Classical period along with formal design and structure.**

Begun in 1767. Robert Adam. Library at Kenwood House. London, England.

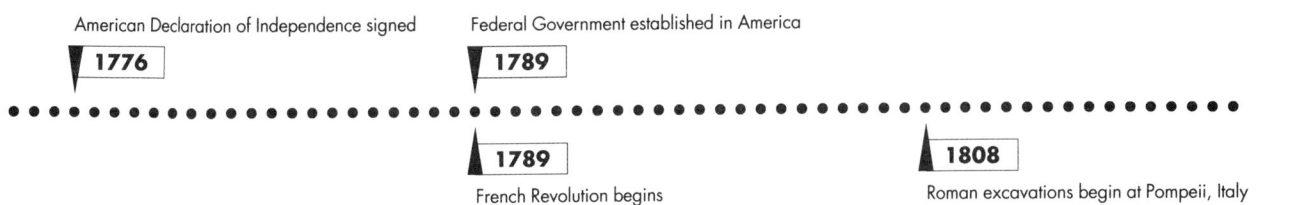

American Declaration of Independence signed
1776

Federal Government established in America
1789

1789
French Revolution begins

1808
Roman excavations begin at Pompeii, Italy

In a Classical concerto, the soloist and the orchestra are equals—another example of the Classical emphasis on balance.

Perhaps the most important instrumental development of the period was the **symphony**, *a large-scale piece for orchestra in three or more movements*. A Classical symphony usually consisted of four movements in this order: 1) A dramatic, fast movement; 2) A slow movement, often in sonata form; 3) A dance-style movement; 4) An exciting, fast movement.

Major Classical Composers

The Classical period was dominated by two composers, Franz Joseph Haydn and Wolfgang Amadeus Mozart. Both were popular and respected musicians in their time, and both remain among the best loved and most widely performed composers of our time. Haydn composed more than 100 symphonies and 68 string quartets, as well as sonatas, operas, masses, and other works. Although Mozart died just before he reached the age of 36, he composed more than 600 musical works, including over 40 symphonies and 20 concertos, which are considered among his greatest achievements.

A third major composer of the time, Ludwig van Beethoven, belongs both to the Classical period and to the next era, the Romantic period. Beethoven's compositions began in Classical style, but the texture, emotion, and new forms of his later music belong more to the Romantic period.

Check Your Understanding

Recall

1. To whom did artists of the Classical period look for standards and ideals?
2. What were the central attitudes of the Classical period?
3. What is chamber music?
4. For which instruments is a string quartet composed?
5. What is a symphony? Which four movements are usually included in a Classical symphony?
6. Who are the two major composers of the Classical period? What kinds of works did each compose?

Thinking It Through

1. Describe a Classical composition you have listened to. What characteristics mark the work as coming from the Classical period?
2. What do you think led Classical composers, other artists, and society in general to want less freedom and more structure?

Classical Period **157**

CLASSICAL CONNECTIONS

Listening to...
Classical Music

CHORAL SELECTION

Mozart— *Don Giovanni*, Act I, "Là Ci Darem la Mano"

Don Giovanni is an opera in two acts. The characters are: Don Giovanni, a young nobleman; Leporello, his servant; the Commendatore Seville; Donna Anna, Seville's daughter; Don Ottavio, her fiancé; Donna Elvira, a lady of Burgos; Zerlina, a country girl; and Masetto, her fiancé.

In this aria, "Là Ci Darem la Mano," Don Giovanni sings to Zerlina, whom he meets at her engagement party. He is interrupted in his flirtatious overtures by the entrance of Donna Elvira, an old flame of his whom he had deserted. In the end of the opera, he receives just retribution for his actions when a supernatural flame destroys him and his palace. Zerlina marries Masetto.

INSTRUMENTAL SELECTION

Mozart— Symphony No. 40 in G Minor, First Movement

Symphony No. 40 was written in sonata form and is an excellent example of the form being followed exactly. This sonata form includes: exposition of a main theme in the tonic or home key, a bridge which modulates to a new key, and then a second theme in a new key. The closing section of this portion is in the key of the second theme. Development of the sonata includes a new treatment of the themes and various modulations, recapitulation with the first theme back in the tonic key, a bridge, a second theme closing in the tonic key, and finally a coda in the tonic key.

CLASSICAL CONNECTIONS

Introducing...

"Sanctus"

Luigi Cherubini

Setting the Stage

Did you ever stop to consider what qualifies a radio favorite as a classic dance tune? Probably the tempo is steady and you feel a definite beat or pulse. (Can you imagine trying to dance to a piece that constantly changed meter? No way!) These same characteristics of deliberate pulsation and a definite feeling of meter were major traits of music from the Classical period. Certainly "Sanctus" is no exception. The piece is marked at ♩ = ca. 116, and the tempo is maintained throughout the piece with only a slight ritard at the end of the selection. The chordal texture is dominant throughout the piece, and we must remember when we sing this selection that the overall tone quality is light without vibrato.

Meeting the Composer

Luigi Cherubini (1760–1842)

Luigi Cherubini (1760–1842) was a famous Italian composer. He studied with his father as a young child, and was a student, subsequently, of Bartolomeo, Alessandro Felici, and Sarti. By the time he was 13 years old, he had already written a mass and a stage-intermezzo for a society theater. He settled in Paris, permanently, in 1788. He was one of the great modern masters of counterpoint, and his scores—especially his sacred music—bear witness to his skill. His works include 15 Italian and 14 French operas, a ballet, 17 cantatas, 14 choruses, 11 solemn masses, and 2 requiems.

CLASSICAL LESSON

Sanctus

Latin Text
COMPOSER: *Luigi Cherubini (1760–1842)*
ARRANGER: *Patrick Liebergen*

CHORAL MUSIC TERMS
Classical
melodic leaps
melodic steps
vocal tone quality

VOICING
SATB

PERFORMANCE STYLE
Energetic and rhythmic
Accompanied by keyboard

FOCUS
- Read and sing melodic leaps with supported tone.
- Sing with bright vocal tone quality.

Warming Up

Vocal Warm-Up

Before you begin singing, turn to a neighbor and give him or her a back rub, gently massaging the neck and shoulder areas. Finish with a light pounding on the back, up and down the spinal area. Reverse roles. Now, sing this exercise using *ha* and *hee*. Use plenty of breath support, and a light vocal tone quality. Move up by half steps as you repeat the exercise.

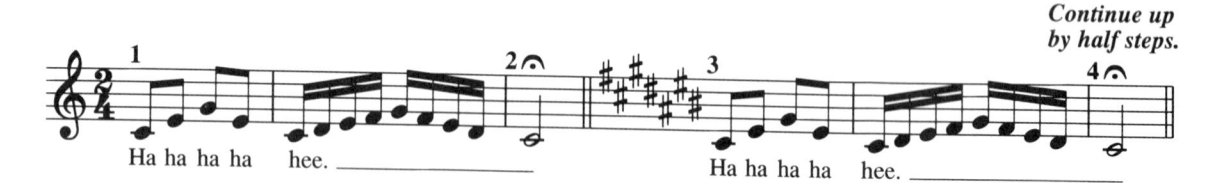

Sight-Singing

Sight-sing this exercise using solfège and hand signs or numbers. Notice the 3/4 meter. Where are the broken chords? Where are the stepwise passages?

160 *Choral Connections Level 3 Mixed Voices*

Singing: "Sanctus"

Almost everyone has some idea of what "Classical" music sounds like. You have learned that this word describes music composed in the Classical period of music history, 1750–1820. What words would you use to describe music of the Classical period? What would the meter, rhythm, melody, tempo, and dynamics be? What mood would it evoke?

Listen to "Sanctus," then tell how it did and did not meet your predictions of music from the Classical period.

Now turn to the music for "Sanctus" on page 162.

HOW DID YOU DO?

Think about your preparation and performance of "Sanctus."

1. Describe your sight-singing ability. What can you do well? What is difficult or needs more work?
2. Describe the mood of "Sanctus," and the vocal tone quality you used. Demonstrate by singing in a quartet or double quartet, choosing part of "Sanctus" that you can do well.
3. How do you tell the difference between melodic steps and leaps visually and aurally? Does a performer do anything different for leaps than steps?
4. Explain why this piece is considered an exemplary model of vocal music of the Classical period. Give specific musical characteristics.

Sanctus

From *Requiem* in C minor

Luigi Cherubini (1760–1842)
Edited and Arranged by Patrick M. Liebergen
English Setting by Patrick M. Liebergen

Four-part Chorus of Mixed Voices with Keyboard

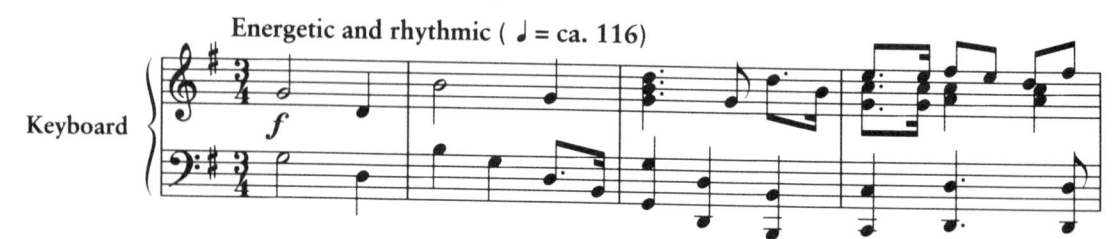

Copyright © 1994 by Carl Fischer, Inc.
International Copyright Secured.
All rights reserved including performing rights.
WARNING! This composition is protected by Copyright law. To photocopy or reproduce
by any method is an infringement of the Copyright law. Anyone who reproduces copyrighted
matter is subject to substantial penalties and assessments for each infringement.
Printed in the U.S.A.

Sanctus

16
tér - ra glό - ri - a, glό - ri - a tú - a. Ho-
heav - en, glo - ry be to God for - ev - er. Ho-
tér - ra glό - ri - a, glό - ri - a tú - a. Ho-
heav - en, glo - ry be to God for - ev - er. Ho-
tér - ra glό - ri - a, glό - ri - a tú - a. Ho-
heav - en, glo - ry be to God for - ev - er. Ho-
tér - ra glό - ri - a, glό - ri - a tú - a. Ho-
heav - en, glo - ry be to God for - ev - er. Ho-
16
20
sán - na, ho - sán - na in ex - cél - sis!
san - na, ho - san - na in the high - est!
sán - na, ho - sán - na in ex - cél - sis!
san - na, ho - san - na in the high - est!
sán - na, ho - sán - na in ex - cél - sis!
san - na, ho - san - na in the high - est!
sub. pp
sán - na, ho - sán - na in ex - cél - sis! Ben - e -
san - na, ho - san - na in the high - est! Praise the
20
sub. pp

Sanctus

166 *Choral Connections* Level 3 Mixed Voices

An episode in the lives of the middle and lower classes of the nineteenth century is reflected in the realism of *Concert in the Tuileries* by Edouard Manet (1832–1883). The realistic treatment is also obvious in the dramatic subject matter that appeared in the operas of the Italian composers of the Romantic period, such as Rossini, Bellini, and Verdi.

1862. Edouard Manet. *Concert in the Tuileries.* (Detail.) Oil on canvas. 75 x 118 cm (30 x 46 ½"). National Gallery, London.

Romantic Period

1820–1900

After completing this lesson, you will be able to:
- Discuss the most important developments of the Romantic period.
- Identify the major musical forms of the Romantic period.
- Explain the importance of nationalism in Romantic music.
- Identify at least three major Romantic composers.

Emotion, imagination, and a concern for the individual returned to the arts with the Romantic period, which defined most of the nineteenth century, from about 1820 until around 1900. A new sense of political and artistic freedom emerged, as artists, including musicians, became impatient with established rules and tradition.

A Time of Freedom and Imagination

In many ways, the Romantic period was a reaction against the constraints of the Classical period. People became less interested in the balance and clarity of earlier times. Rather, their interests focused on adventure, a love of nature, and freedom of expression.

The Romantic period coincided with the Industrial Revolution, which created many new nonagricultural jobs and contributed to the growth of cities. The middle class grew in numbers, as well as in confidence and power. More and more people took an active part in their culture and their nation. A new sense of patriotism grew among citizens of individual European countries and of the United States.

Visual artists of the Romantic period reflected the era's attitudes with bolder, more colorful works. The enthusiasm for nature was reflected in the growing popularity of landscape paintings. The Romantic paintings of William Turner and John Constable express the movements and moods of nature. Later, Impressionist painters, including Edouard Manet, Claude Monet, and Pierre Auguste Renoir, developed new techniques to bring the sense and feeling of nature alive for the viewer.

Romantic Musical Developments

Romantic composers worked primarily with the same forms that had developed and become popular during the Classical period. However, Romantic composers treated these forms in ways that made new statements about music and about their own attitudes toward life. Romantic compositions, focused on both the heights and depths of human emotion, were characterized by complexity, exploration, and excitement. The interests of the period were expressed in larger, more complex vocal melodies and more colorful harmonies. In addition, instrumentation was expanded to enhance the overall possibilities of tone color in the music, and the rhythms became more free and more flexible.

COMPOSERS
Ludwig van Beethoven (1770–1827)
Franz Schubert (1797–1828)
Hector Berlioz (1803–1869)
Felix Mendelssohn (1809–1847)
Frédéric Chopin (1810–1849)
Robert Schumann (1810–1856)
Franz Liszt (1811–1886)
Richard Wagner (1813–1883)
Giuseppe Verdi (1813–1901)
Clara Schumann (1819–1896)
Johann Strauss (1825–1899)
Johannes Brahms (1833–1897)
Peter Ilyich Tschaikovsky (1840–1893)
Giacomo Puccini (1858–1924)

ARTISTS
Élisabeth Vigée-Lebrun (1755–1842)
Joseph Mallard William Turner (1775–1851)
John Constable (1776–1837)
Rosa Bonheur (1822–1899)
Edouard Manet (1832–1883)
James A. McNeill Whistler (1834–1903)
Edgar Degas (1834–1917)
Paul Cezanne (1839–1906)
Claude Monet (1840–1926)
Berthe Morisot (1841–1895)
Pierre Auguste Renoir (1841–1919)
Mary Cassatt (1845–1926)
Vincent van Gogh (1853–1890)
Georges Seurat (1859–1891)

AUTHORS
Noah Webster (1758–1843)
Sir Walter Scott (1771–1832)
Mary Wollstonecraft Shelley (1797–1851)
Ralph Waldo Emerson (1803–1882)
Elizabeth Barrett Browning (1806–1861)
Leo Tolstoy (1828–1910)

CHORAL MUSIC TERMS
art song
music critic
nationalism

Louisiana Purchase
transacted | **1803**

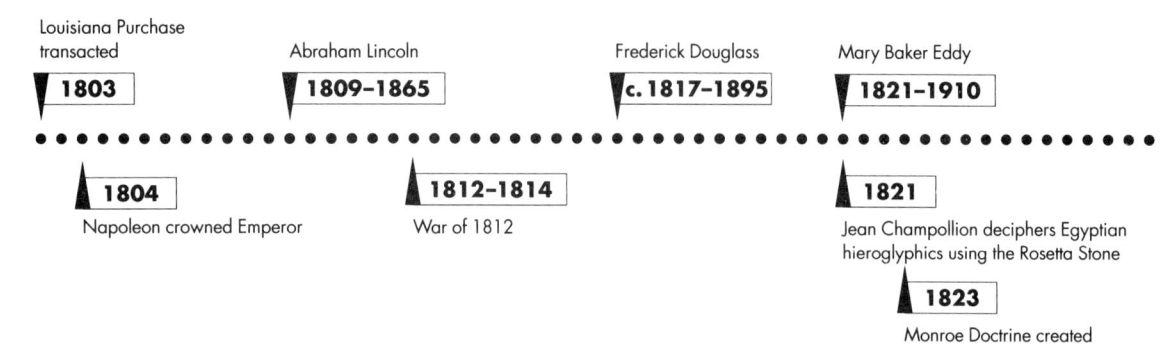

1804 Napoleon crowned Emperor

Abraham Lincoln | **1809–1865**

1812–1814 War of 1812

Frederick Douglass | **c. 1817–1895**

Mary Baker Eddy | **1821–1910**

1821 Jean Champollion deciphers Egyptian hieroglyphics using the Rosetta Stone

1823 Monroe Doctrine created

Many Romantic compositions reflect the period's spirit of **nationalism**, *pride in a country's historical and legendary past.* Composers used traditional legends, as well as nationalistic dramas and novels, as the basis for both vocal and instrumental works.

Nationalism is seen perhaps most clearly in the operas of Richard Wagner and Giuseppe Verdi. Wagner's works, including the series of four operas known as *The Ring of the Nibelung*, are based on epic sagas and are intended to preserve German legends and folk music. Verdi, who has become the most popular of all opera composers, emphasized the importance of following Italian historical and cultural traditions.

Other musical forms of the Romantic period also reflect the era's nationalism. There was an increased interest in the traditional folk tunes and folk dances of specific nations or regions; these folk tunes were often used or imitated in serious compositions. German folk songs can be heard in Robert Schumann's piano pieces and symphonies, for example. In the United States, the songs composed by Stephen Foster express his understanding of and special pride in the southern United States.

As the Romantic period progressed, the most important vocal form became the **art song**, *an expressive song about life, love, and human relationships for solo voice and piano.* Art songs are known in German as *lieder*, and the most famous composers of these Romantic works were German-speakers. Austrian Franz Schubert composed more than 600 songs, as well as symphonies, string quartets, and other works, before his death at the age of 31. German composers Robert Schumann and Johannes Brahms are also known for their *lieder*.

Instrumental music became more elaborate and expressive during the Romantic period. Symphonies gained in popularity. Symphony orchestras increased in size, and percussion held a new place of importance. The most famous symphonies of the period—and perhaps of all time—are those composed by Ludwig van Beethoven. Some symphonies, including Beethoven's *Ninth Symphony*, added a chorus to the instrumental music.

Dance music also grew in importance during this time. Great social occasions became popular and required new dance compositions. The waltzes of Johann Strauss were played throughout Europe; new polonaises and other dance forms were also composed.

Modern Innovations of the Romantic Period

During the Romantic period, musicians and other artists received less support from wealthy or aristocratic patrons. As a result, composers began to think about "selling" their music to an audience. For several Romantic musicians, a colorful and controversial private life was part of "the package"; it sparked public interest in the composer and his works.

Another innovation of the period was the emergence of the **music critic**, *a writer who explains composers and their music to the public and who helps set standards in musical taste.* As music became more diverse and as increasing numbers of people listened to and appreciated new compositions, critics often sought to guide the direction new music might take.

Mary Mason Lyon founds Mt. Holyoke Female Seminary
1837

American Civil War
1861–1865

Wireless telegraph developed by Guglielmo Marconi
1895

1835–1910 Mark Twain

1844–1900 Friedrich Nietzsche

1889 Jane Addams and Ellen Starr found Hull House

1898 Motion picture camera patented by Thomas Edison; sound recording developed

▲ John Nash (1752–1835) reaches for originality in his design of the Royal Pavilion in Brighton, England. The combination of Oriental onion domes and minarets with an interior in the Classical style is totally unique. Interest in the exotic was also a hallmark of Romantic composers who dealt with foreign lands as well as legends and mysticism in their works.

1815–23. John Nash. Royal Pavilion, Brighton, England.

Check Your Understanding

Recall

1. In what ways was the Romantic period a reaction against the Classical period?

2. What is nationalism? How is it important in Romantic music?

3. What are art songs? Which Romantic composers are especially noted for this kind of composition?

4. How did symphonies change during the Romantic period?

5. Why did composers of the Romantic period have to start thinking about "selling" their music to an audience?

6. What is a music critic?

Thinking It Through

1. Review what you know about the musical ideals of the Renaissance period, the Baroque period, the Classical period, and the Romantic period. What cycle or trend can you identify? What implications do you think that cycle or trend might have?

2. What relationship do you think might exist between the decline of the patronage system and the emergence of the music critic?

ROMANTIC CONNECTIONS

Listening to...
Romantic Music

CHORAL SELECTION

Verdi — *Rigoletto*, Act III, "La donna è mobile"

Giuseppe Verdi (1813–1901) is considered the foremost Italian opera composer during the Romantic era. He is famous for expressive vocal melodies and many of his melodies are known throughout the world. In R*igoletto*, Verdi chose a hunchbacked court jester as the main character. Rigoletto, the hunchback, is of questionable character but has a deep love for his daughter, Gilda. Rigoletto tries to protect her from the Duke of Mantua, a womanizer. Gilda eventually falls in love with the Duke and Rigoletto swears to avenge his daughter. In Act III, Rigoletto hires an assassin to kill the Duke. Gilda interferes in her father's plan and is killed instead. As Rigoletto is dragging the body bag that he thinks bears the dead body of his sworn enemy, he hears the Duke singing "La donna è mobile." He soon realizes that in the bag is actually his beloved daughter, Gilda.

INSTRUMENTAL SELECTION

Berlioz — *Symphonie fantastique*, Fourth Movement, "March to the Scaffold"

Hector Berlioz (1803–1869) is a famous French Romantic composer known for experimenting with orchestral sounds. During his time, the music establishment thought Berlioz was unconventional and sometimes irritating. In *Symphonie fantastique*, Berlioz uses an *idée fixe*, or fixed idea, throughout all five movements.

The recurrence of the same melody throughout five movements was a novel idea in Berlioz's day. In the fourth movement, "March to the Scaffold," the character dreams he is being led to his execution. The *fixed idea* returns before the guillotine's final blow as the character is thinking of his beloved.

ROMANTIC CONNECTIONS

Introducing...
"If I Should See You All Alone"

Felix Mendelssohn

Setting the Stage

This German folk song setting is an example of the Nationalistic style that was popular during the Romantic period. The song has an idealized romantic text of undying and profound love, and is set in intimate 3/4 meter, with skipping rhythms like the leaping of the heart. The phrasing and repetition of text also enhances understanding of the piece. Through melodic line, dynamic contrast, and alternation of open and closed harmonies, the sense of protection and devotion is heightened.

Meeting the Composer
Felix Mendelssohn (1809–1847)

Felix Mendelssohn was born in Hamburg, Germany, in 1809. He was acclaimed as a fine pianist and conductor, and toured England. Although he died an early death at the age of 38, Mendelssohn's place in history is assured because of his compositions, his teaching at the Leipzig Conservatory, which he founded, and especially his rediscovery and performance of Bach's music.

ROMANTIC LESSON

If I Should See You All Alone

CHORAL MUSIC TERMS
dotted rhythm
key
key signature
3/4 meter
tonal center

German Folk Song
COMPOSER: *Felix Mendelssohn (1809–1847)*
ARRANGER: *Richard Williamson*

VOICING
SAB

PERFORMANCE STYLE
Tenderly
Accompanied by piano

FOCUS
- Read and clap rhythms in 3/4 meter including dotted rhythms.
- Sight-sing in a major key.
- Identify key signatures for major keys.

Warming Up

Vocal Warm-Up

First clap the rhythm of this exercise. Notice the dotted rhythms. Next sing the exercise using solfège and hand signs or numbers. Keep the rhythm and pitches accurate. Move up or down by half steps.

Finally, conduct in 3/4 meter as you sing, using both arms mirroring each other. This will help loosen your upper body.

What key does this exercise begin in? How do you know?

Sight-Singing

Review this exercise in your head before singing it. Look for trouble spots. Now sight-sing using solfège and hand signs or numbers, repeating if necessary. Advanced readers are encouraged to conduct while reading.

Singing: "If I Should See You All Alone"

Do you have any recordings or tapes in your collection that are "typically romantic"? Many songs like this have a very singable melody, one that sticks in your mind all day.

Mendelssohn wrote "If I Should See You All Alone" over a hundred years ago, but it is one of those typically romantic catchy tunes. Its music is bonded with the words to express the meaning as the words alone cannot do. There are soaring dynamics and soft delicate sounds which contrast to intensify the expression—again typically romantic, and an excellent example of vocal music of the Romantic period.

Now turn to the music for "If I Should See You All Alone" on page 176.

HOW DID YOU DO?

Even a good tune requires skill to be performed effectively. Think about your preparation and performance of "If I Should See You All Alone."

1. Tell how 3/4 meter works, and then sing and conduct the Sight-Singing exercise to demonstrate your skill.
2. How do dotted rhythms work? Sing the phrase beginning at measure 25 to demonstrate your skill at performing dotted rhythms.
3. Describe the key in which this piece is written. How do you know what key it is in?
4. Describe why this piece is considered an exemplary model of Romantic vocal music. Give specific musical characteristics.

If I Should See You All Alone

(Folk Song)

Felix Mendelssohn
Arranged by Richard Williamson

Three-part Chorus of Mixed Voices
with Piano Accompaniment

Soprano, Alto

If I should see you all a-lone out in the storm, out in the storm, Then with my coat I'd cov-er you___ and keep you warm, and keep you warm. And if the storms of sad-ness come to

O säh' ich auf der Hai-de dort im Stur-me dich, im Stur-me dich! Mit mei-nem Man-tel vor dem Sturm___ be-schützt' ich dich, be-schützt' ich dich. Und kommt mit sei-nem Stur-me je dir

©1994 Music 70 Music Publishers
All Rights Reserved
International Copyright Secured
Printed in U.S.A.

If I Should See You All Alone **177**

26
des - ert land so dry and bare, so dry and bare, It
Wü - ste, die so braun und dürr, so braun und dürr, Zum
des - ert land so dry and bare, so dry and bare, It
Wü - ste, die so braun und dürr, so braun und dürr, Zum
29
p
would be par - a - dise to me if you were there, if
Pa - ra - die - se wür - de sie, wär'st du bei mir, wär'st
p
would be par - a - dise to me if you were there, if
Pa - ra - die - se wür - de sie, wär'st du bei mir, wär'st
p
32
cresc.
you were there. If all the rich - es of the world were
du bei mir, Und wär ein Kö - nig ich und wär' die
cresc.
you were there. If all the rich - es of the world were
du bei mir, Und wär ein Kö - nig ich und wär' die
p
cresc.

If I Should See You All Alone

▲ **Individuals in contemporary society are increasingly interested in expressing their ethnic backgrounds. Palmer Hayden shows this interest by juxtaposing the comedy, tragedy, and pleasures of the African-American painter who works during the day as a janitor, yet aspires to be a great artist. Music of the twentieth century is influenced by many different cultures as well as by technology and experimentation.**

1937. Palmer Hayden. *The Janitor Who Paints*. Oil on canvas. 99.4 x 83.5 cm (39 1/8 x 32 7/8"). National Museum of American Art, Washington, D.C.

Contemporary Period

1900–Present

After completing this lesson, you will be able to:
- *Identify technological advancements that have affected the involvement of the general public in the music of the Contemporary period.*
- *Discuss at least five musical developments of the Contemporary period.*
- *Identify at least four Contemporary composers.*
- *Explain the importance of fusion in Contemporary music.*

COMPOSERS

Richard Strauss (1864–1949)
Ralph Vaughan Williams (1872–1958)
Arnold Schoenberg (1874–1951)
Charles Ives (1874–1954)
Béla Bartók (1881–1945)
Igor Stravinsky (1882–1971)
Sergei Prokofiev (1891–1953)
Paul Hindemith (1895–1963)
George Gershwin (1898–1937)
Aaron Copland (1900–1990)
Samuel Barber (1910–1981)
Gian Carlo Menotti (1911–)
Benjamin Britten (1913–1976)
Leonard Bernstein (1918–1990)
Philip Glass (1937–)
John Rutter (1945–)

ARTISTS

Henri Rousseau (1844–1910)
Edvard Munch (1863–1944)
Wassily Kandinsky (1866–1944)
Henri Matisse (1869–1954)
Pablo Picasso (1881–1973)
Georgia O'Keeffe (1887–1986)
Palmer Hayden (1890–1973)
Jackson Pollock (1912–1956)
Andrew Wyeth (1917–)
Andy Warhol (1930–1987)

AUTHORS

George Bernard Shaw (1856–1950)
Sir Arthur Conan Doyle (1859–1930)
Edith Wharton (1862–1937)
William Faulkner (1897–1962)
Maya Angelou (1928–)

CHORAL MUSIC TERMS

abstract
aleatoric music
dissonance
Expressionism
fusion
Impressionism
twelve-tone music

The twentieth century has been a period of rapid change. The developments in transportation may typify the rate at which change has taken place in all aspects of modern life. In 1900, the first automobiles were coming into use, and the first successful airplane was yet to be built. Today, highways are jammed with automobiles, commercial flights take off regularly from large and small airports, and unmanned spaceflights explore the farthest reaches of the solar system.

Political events have brought repeated and often radical changes in the lives and ideas of people around the world. Among the major political events of the twentieth century have been two world wars, many localized wars, revolutions in Russia and China, the Great Depression, the Cold War, and the rise and fall of communism in many countries. All these changes and more have been part of the Contemporary period, the time from 1900 to right now.

Technology and Contemporary Music

Technological advancements have affected many aspects of twentieth-century life, including the musical interests and involvement of the general public. First, phonographs and records made music readily available to everyone who wanted to hear it. Then, radio brought live musical performances and a wide variety of musical recordings into people's homes. By now, television has replaced radio as a source of news and entertainment—including news about music and musical entertainment—in most homes. Audiotapes, CDs, and computers with interactive software have also become popular, bringing higher quality sounds and images to the public. In addition, synthesizers now make it easier and less expensive for everyone to become involved in making and listening to music.

During the Contemporary period, music and musicians have had to rely much more on the general public for support than during any past time. Composers or musicians may still be employed by reli-

Contemporary Period **181**

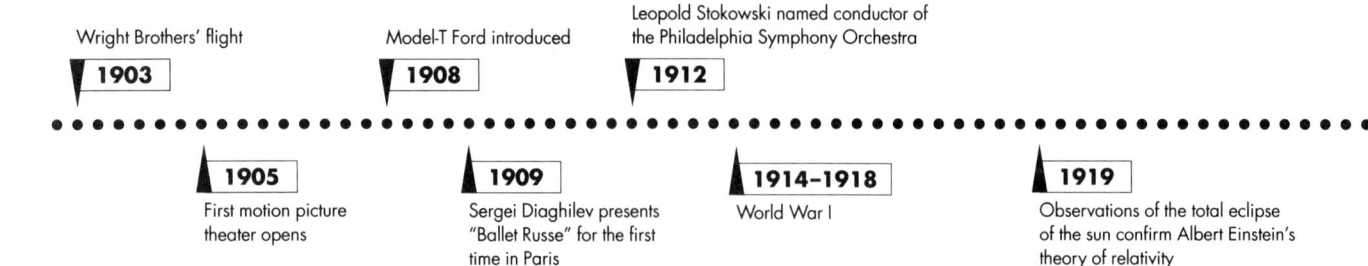

Wright Brothers' flight **1903**	Model-T Ford introduced **1908**	Leopold Stokowski named conductor of the Philadelphia Symphony Orchestra **1912**		
1905 First motion picture theater opens	**1909** Sergei Diaghilev presents "Ballet Russe" for the first time in Paris	**1914–1918** World War I	**1919** Observations of the total eclipse of the sun confirm Albert Einstein's theory of relativity	

gious organizations, city orchestras, or schools, but most support themselves through the sale of concert tickets, published music, and professional recordings. Music also receives some support from nonprofit organizations, but the era of the patronage system is clearly over.

Musical Developments of the Contemporary Period

The twentieth century has been a time of musical changes. Many composers have continued to use forms from the Romantic period, such as the opera, symphony, and art song, but they have adapted these forms to express new musical ideas. Many compositions from the early part of the century are considered **Impressionism**, *works that create a musical picture with a dreamy quality through chromaticism.* Many later works are considered examples of **Expressionism**, *bold and dynamic musical expression of mood with great dissonance.*

Composers of the Contemporary period have experimented with many different approaches to music. Some have worked in an objective style, creating works that stress music for its own sake. Their compositions are **abstract**, *focusing on lines, rows, angles, clusters, textures, and form.*

Many composers have also experimented with music that lacks a tonal center and a scale-oriented organization of pitch. Rather than using traditional chords built on intervals of a third, these modern compositions feature **dissonance**, *chords using seconds, fourths, fifths, and sevenths.*

Another new development is **twelve-tone music**. In this organization, *the twelve tones of the chromatic scale are arranged in a tone row, then the piece is composed by arranging and rearranging the "row" in different ways—backward, forward, in clusters of three or four pitches, and so on.* Twelve-tone compositions can be approached mathematically, and the possible combinations are nearly limitless, especially when arrangements are layered, instrument over instrument. Although this approach to composition fascinates some composers, not all listeners find the resulting works satisfying.

Some Contemporary composers have also created **aleatoric**—or chance—**music**, *works that have only a beginning and an end, with the rest left to chance.* An aleatoric work usually does have a score, but each performer is given the freedom to make many choices, including which pitch to begin on, how long to hold each pitch, how fast to play, and when to stop playing.

Other compositional elements of the Contemporary period include more angular contour of the melody, different concepts of harmony, which may emphasize dissonance, complex rhythms, and specific performance markings. These musical innovations are most evident in the secular music of the twentieth century, but they can be seen in many sacred works as well. The number of sacred compositions has decreased

| First complete talking film **1928** | Television begins under commercial license **1939** | First atomic bomb exploded **1945** |

| **1927** Lindbergh's solo flight across the Atlantic | **1929** New York stock market collapses; Great Depression begins | **1939-1945** World War II | **1950-1953** Korean War |

▲ Just as new compositional techniques in various formats are prevalent in Contemporary music, the architecture in the Opera House in Sydney, Australia, incorporated new materials and construction techniques. Award-winning Danish architect Jørn Utzon (1918–) called for segmented, precast concrete in the construction of the white tiled shells that form the roof of this imaginative and poetic building.

1959–72. Jørn Utzon. Opera House, Sydney, Australia.

during this century. However, important Contemporary musicians, including Leonard Bernstein, Paul Hindemith, Benjamin Britten, Charles Ives, and Gian Carlo Menotti, have composed masses, sacred cantatas, chorales, and othe religious works.

A New Mix

Rapid improvements in communication and transportation have brought people from all parts of the world into closer touch with one another. Individuals and groups have shared many aspects of their cultures, including traditional musical techniques and new musical developments. One of the results of this sharing is **fusion**, *a blending*

Contemporary Period **183**

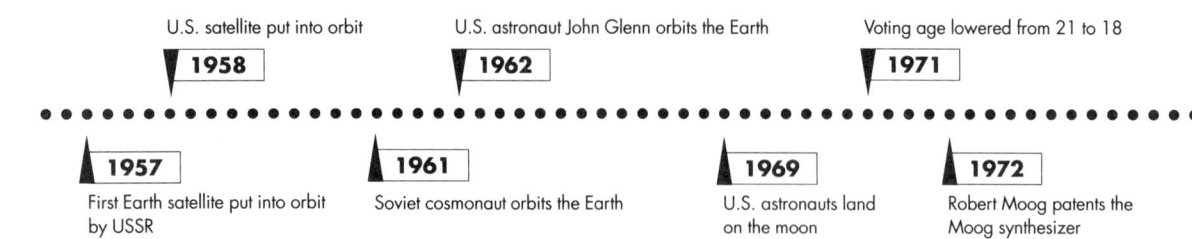

1957	1958	1961	1962	1969	1971	1972
First Earth satellite put into orbit by USSR	U.S. satellite put into orbit	Soviet cosmonaut orbits the Earth	U.S. astronaut John Glenn orbits the Earth	U.S. astronauts land on the moon	Voting age lowered from 21 to 18	Robert Moog patents the Moog synthesizer

of musical styles. Tejano music, for example, is a blending of Mexican and Country styles; zydeco is a blending of African-American, Cajun, and French Canadian styles.

The Contemporary period has also been a time of fusion between popular music styles and art music. Pop singers occasionally perform with professional orchestras and choirs, and opera singers record popular songs and traditional folk music.

Many new kinds of popular music have emerged during the Contemporary period. Some, including blues, jazz, country, rock, and reggae, continue to thrive and to blend with other kinds of popular music. Other styles, such as ragtime, seem to have become part of history rather than popular culture. Popular music styles are part of the change characteristic of the period, and new styles will continue to develop.

The Future of Music

The changes of the Contemporary period are ongoing, and the music of the period continues to evolve. Which trends will prove most significant? When will a new direction emerge that will mark the end of this period? What name will future historians give to the time we call Contemporary? As a consumer of music—and perhaps even as a music maker—you may help determine the answers to these questions.

Check Your Understanding

Recall

1. What is Impressionism?
2. What is abstract music?
3. What is dissonance?
4. List at least three choices that are left up to performers of aleatoric music.
5. What is the status of sacred music in the Contemporary period?
6. What is fusion? Give at least two examples of fusion.

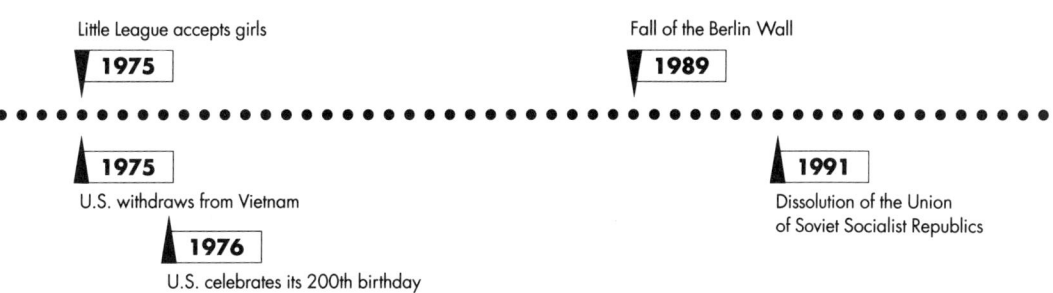

1975 — Little League accepts girls
1975 — U.S. withdraws from Vietnam
1976 — U.S. celebrates its 200th birthday
1989 — Fall of the Berlin Wall
1991 — Dissolution of the Union of Soviet Socialist Republics

Thinking It Through

1. How do you think the change from a patronage system to a reliance on public support has affected the development of music? Explain your ideas.

2. What forms of Contemporary music do you like best? Why? Be specific.

3. Which previous period—Renaissance, Baroque, Classical, or Romantic—do you consider most like the Contemporary period? What similarities can you identify? What do you consider the most important differences?

CONTEMPORARY CONNECTIONS

Listening to...
Contemporary Music

CHORAL SELECTION

Bernstein — "Tonight" from *West Side Story*

West Side Story is a modern-day version of Shakespeare's *Romeo and Juliet*, set in the slums of New York. It deals with the conflict between gang rivalry and youthful love. The plot revolves around a fight ("rumble") between two gangs and the doomed love of its principal characters, Tony and Maria. Tony is shot and dies in Maria's arms.

INSTRUMENTAL SELECTION

Copland — Theme and Variations on "Simple Gifts" from *Appalachian Spring*, Section 7

Aaron Copland (1900–1990), a leading American composer, was born in Brooklyn, New York, to Russian-Jewish immigrant parents. He wanted to write music that would be specifically American in character, so he often drew on American folklore. *Appalachian Spring* originated as a ballet score for the dance choreographer Martha Graham. It is a story about a pioneer celebration in spring around a newly built farmhouse in the Pennsylvania hills. Copland used the Shaker melody, "Simple Gifts," as a folk tune in the score. Section 7 accompanies "scenes of daily activity for the husband and wife."

CONTEMPORARY CONNECTIONS

Introducing...
"Still, Still, Still"

John Rutter

Meeting the Arranger
John Rutter

John Rutter was born in 1945 in London, where he first learned music as part of a boys' chorus. He and his fellow choristers performed the first recording of Benjamin Britten's *War Requiem*, conducted by Britten and featuring famous soloists of the time. The experience proved to be inspirational for the young Rutter. Pursuing his music studies at Cambridge, he conducted his first recording while still an undergraduate student. Soon after, a large-scale choral and orchestral piece of Rutter's was premiered at the university.

Following these auspicious beginnings, Rutter's compositional career has been broad and far-reaching—he has composed both large- and small-scale choral works, various orchestral and instrumental pieces, a piano concerto, two children's operas, and music for BBC television. Three of his works—*Christmas Night-Carols of the Nativity*, *Requiem*, and *Gloria*—have sold over 100,000 copies.

Currently, Rutter runs his own record label, *Collegium*, one of the most successful independent music companies in Britain. *Collegium* has produced several albums by the Cambridge Singers, a popular mixed-voice choir that Rutter directs. In addition to these involvements in his native country, Rutter spends much of his time in the United States, where he has become something of a TV personality, and a requested speaker and conductor at universities, churches, music festivals, and conferences.

CONTEMPORARY LESSON

Still, Still, Still

German Folk Song
ARRANGER: John Rutter

CHORAL MUSIC TERMS
contemporary
dynamic contrast
intonation

VOICING
SATB

PERFORMANCE STYLE
Sweetly
A cappella

FOCUS
- Hum with energy and accurate intonation.
- Sing with dynamic contrast.

Warming Up

Vocal Warm-Up
Sing this Vocal Warm-Up with buzzing lips—lip trills. Keep the pitches accurate. Continue up by half steps.

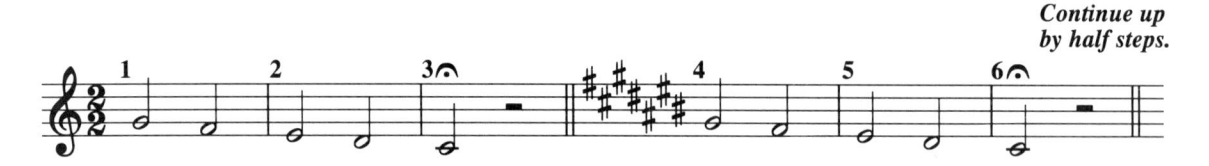

Sight-Singing
Sight-sing these pitches using solfège and hand signs or numbers. Can you read it correctly the first time? Listen to the chords and tune them carefully. Repeat this exercise *ppp*, *pp*, *p*, *mp*, *mf*, *f*, and *ff* (but don't yell).

188 *Choral Connections   Level 3 Mixed Voices*

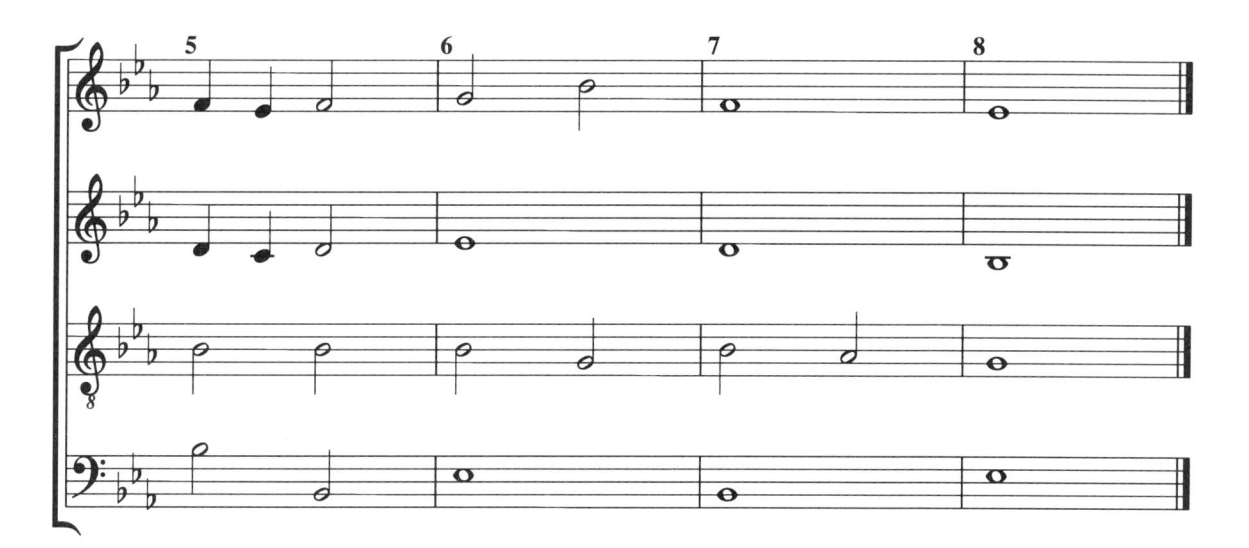

Singing: "Still, Still, Still"

How well can you hum? Here are the steps to better humming:

- Pinch the bridge of your nose and hum—feel the resonant tones. How do you think you can get maximum amount of energy and sound out of your hum?

- Sing a series of vowels (*oh* or *ah*) into your rounded hands, and feel the buzzing sensation.

- Keep this sensation as you withdraw your hands from your mouth.

- Continue singing, but gradually close your lips until they are barely touching, and sing the following:

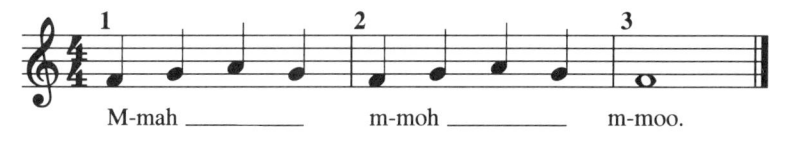

M-mah _____ m-moh _____ m-moo.

- Sight-sing measures 5–16 of "Still, Still, Still" on the vowel *o*, remembering the buzzing.

- Repeat, but gently close the lips, remembering to sing *oh* behind closed lips.

- Use lots of breath support to keep in tune.

Now turn to the music for "Still, Still, Still" on page 190.

HOW DID YOU DO?

Think about your preparation and performance of "Still, Still, Still."

1. Describe how to get the maximum sound from your hum, and then demonstrate.

2. Describe the dynamics in "Still, Still, Still." Perform the piece with a small group, demonstrating your skill at using dynamic contrast.

3. Is this piece a good example of contemporary vocal music? Why? Why not? Can any piece be a good example of contemporary vocal music?

Still, Still, Still

German Carol
Arranged by John Rutter
Words translated from the German
by John Rutter

Mixed Voices, SATB (div.), A cappella

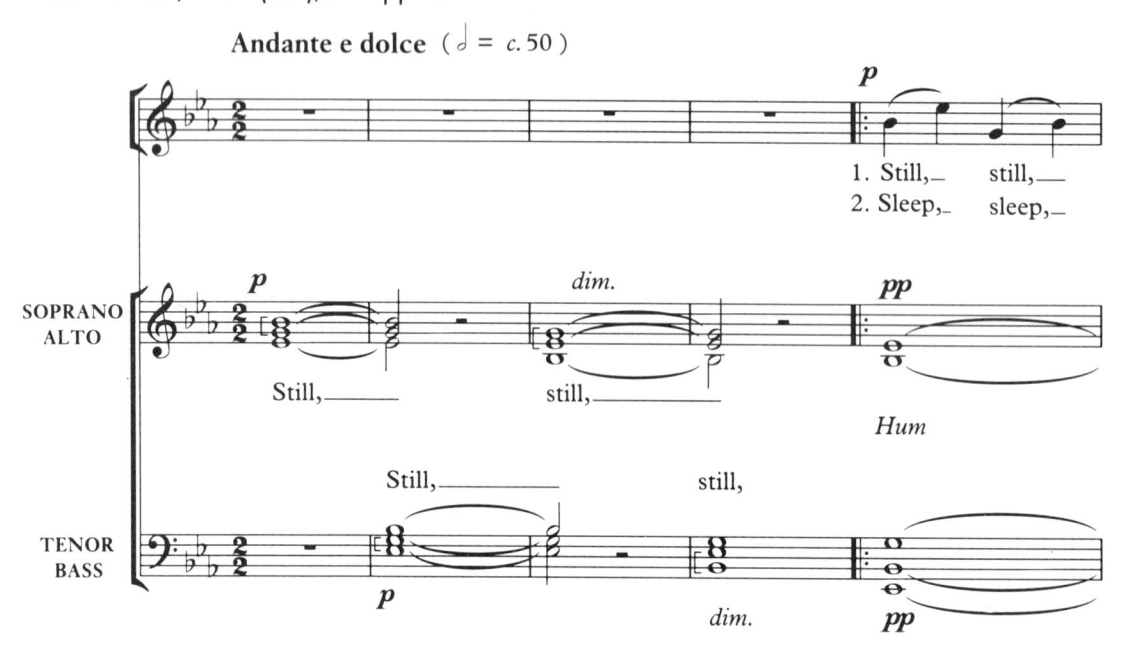

Andante e dolce ($\quarter = c.\,50$)

1. Still, still, still: The night is calm and still. The Christ child in his
2. Sleep, sleep, sleep: Sweet Jesus, softly sleep, While Mary sings and

Still, still,
Hum

Still, still,

*These solos may instead be sung by a semi-chorus.

Copyright © 1994 by Hinshaw Music, Inc.,
P.O. Box 470, Chapel Hill, N.C. 27514
International Copyright Secured. All rights reserved.
Copying or reproducing this publication in whole or in part
violates the Federal Copyright Law.

Reprinted by Permission.

crib lies sleeping, Angels round him watch are keeping.
gently holds you, Safely in her arms enfolds you.

Still, still, still: The night is calm and still.
Sleep, sleep, sleep: Sweet Jesus, softly sleep.

3. Joy, joy, joy; Glad tidings of great joy! For,

Glad tidings of joy!

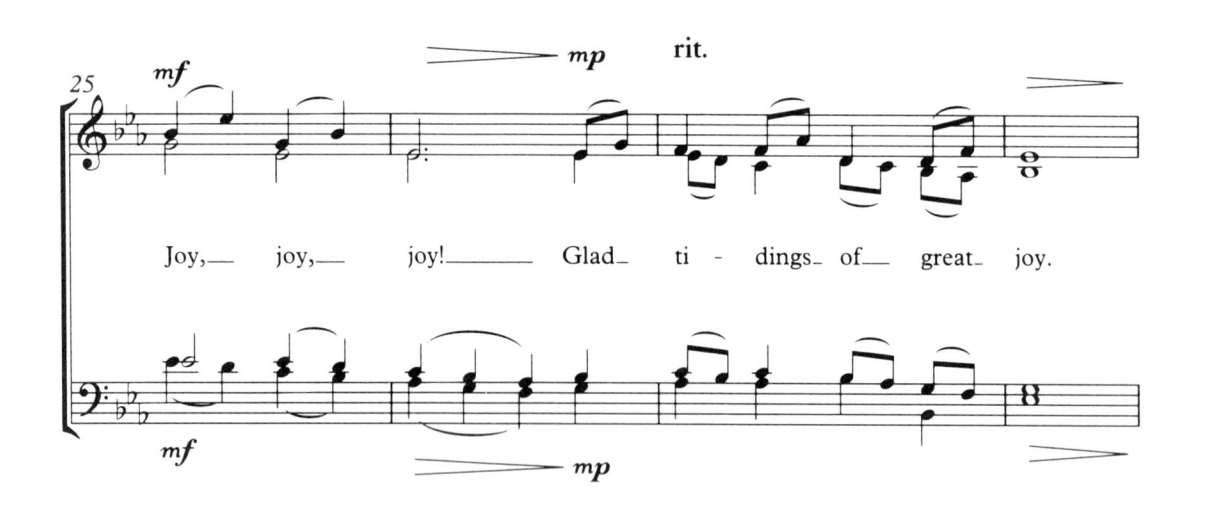

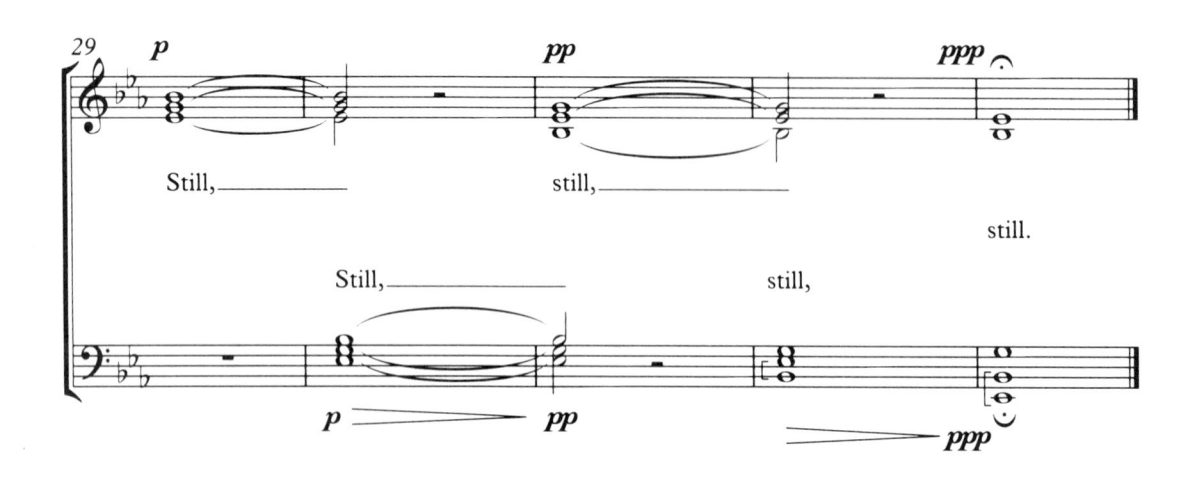

through God's ho-ly in-car-na-tion, Christ is born for our sal-va-tion.

Joy, joy, joy! Glad ti-dings of great joy.

Still, still, still.

Still, still,

Additional Performance Selections

WARM-UPS FOR PERFORMANCE SELECTIONS

VOICING
SATB

PERFORMANCE STYLE
Moderately, Latin feel
Accompanied by claves, drum, and temple blocks

Shut De Dō

Warming Up

Vocal Warm-Up

Sing this exercise on *ho*. Notice the syncopation, and sing in a percussive style. Move up by half steps on each repeat.

Continue up by half steps.

Ho ho ho ho. Ho ho ho ho.

Now turn to page **197.**

VOICING
SATB

PERFORMANCE STYLE
Moderate, gospel style.
Accompanied by piano, optional guitar, bass, and drums

The River

Warming Up

Vocal Warm-Up

As you sing this exercise on *bluh*, loosen up the upper part of your body (shoulders, neck, arms, wrist, hands, and jaw). Move up or down a half step on each repeat.

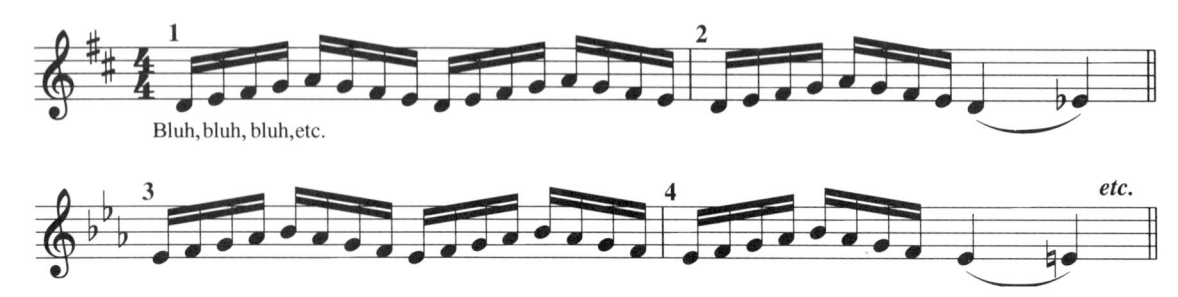

Bluh, bluh, bluh, etc.

etc.

Now turn to page **204.**

194 *Choral Connections   Level 3 Mixed Voices*

VOICING
SATB

PERFORMANCE STYLE
Brightly
A cappella

Look-A That Star

Warming Up

Vocal Warm-Up
Sing these chord progressions on *doo*. Notice the syncopation in the second measure, and sing the rhythm crisply. Move up by half steps on each repeat.

Continue up by half steps.

Doo doo doo doo   doo doo doo doo.

Now turn to page **210.**

VOICING
SATB

PERFORMANCE STYLE
Gently
Accompanied by piano

A Holiday Wish

Warming Up

Vocal Warm-Up
Sing the exercise using the cheerful holiday text. Move a half step up on each repetition. Notice the tonic leap from *so* to high *do*, then the descending stepwise scale pattern. Think of another seasonal text to use that incorporates different vowels on each syllable.

Hap - py — hol - i - days.

Now turn to page **217.**

Warm-Ups for Performance Selections   **195**

VOICING
SATB

PERFORMANCE STYLE
Latin style
A cappella

El Progreso Honduras

Warming Up

Vocal Warm-Up

Sing this pattern using solfège and hand signs or numbers until the intervals and rhythms are comfortable. Notice that the tonal center is *so*, giving the melody a modal feeling.

Now turn to page **223**.

Shut De Dō

Words and Music by
Randy Stonehill
Arranged by Mark Hayes

Moderately ♩ = 84
Latin feel

Continue rhythm in similar pattern
Unis. **TENORS**

Shut de dō, keep out de dev-il.

Shut de dō, keep de dev-il in the night.

Shut de dō, keep out de dev-il.

Light de can-dle, ev-'ry-thin's al-right.

©1983 by Stonehillian Music (adm. by WORD, INC.)
All Rights Reserved. Used by Permission.

198 Choral Connections Level 3 Mixed Voices

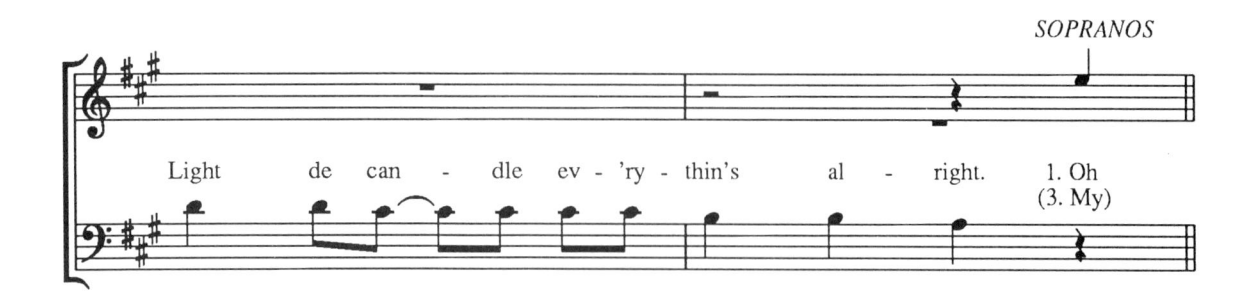

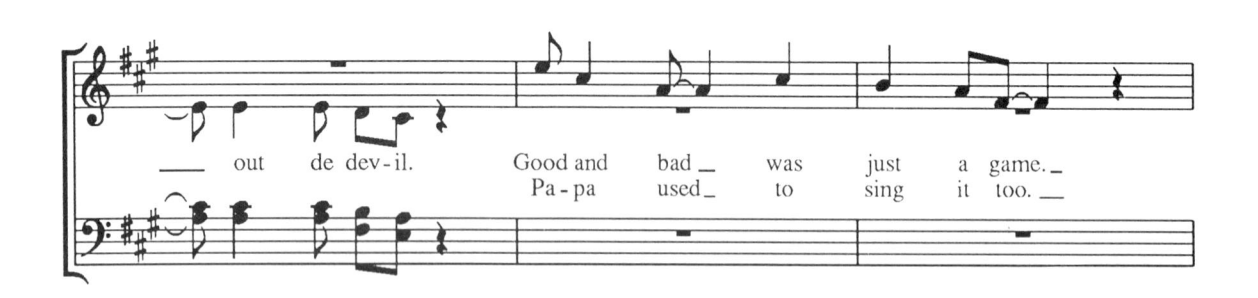

proved to me they're not the same.
so I sing this song for you.
I say
Shut de dō, keep de dev - il in the night.
C
Shut de-dō, keep out de dev-il. Shut de dō, keep de
de dō de dev - il
dev - il in the night. Shut de dō, keep out de dev-il.
de dō de dev - il
3rd time to
Light de can - dle, ev - 'ry - thin's al - right. Light de can - dle, ev - 'ry-

thin's al-right. 2. Oh Satan is an e-vil charm-er.

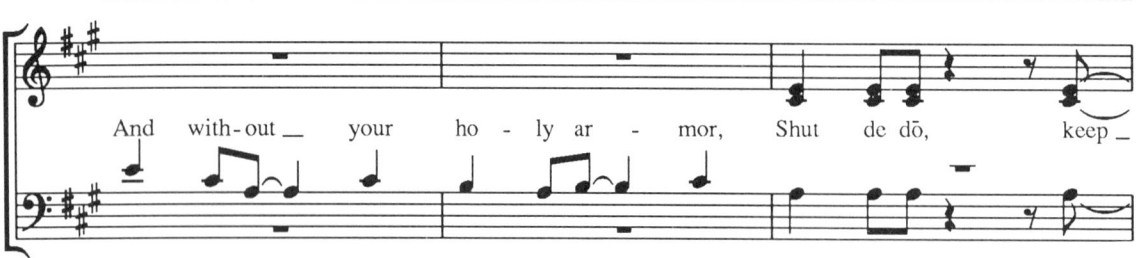

Shut de dō, keep out de dev-il. He's hun-gry for a soul to hurt. Shut de dō, keep de dev-il in the night. And with-out your ho-ly ar-mor, Shut de dō, keep out de dev-il. He will eat you for des-sert!

Shut De Dō **201**

202 *Choral Connections Level 3 Mixed Voices*

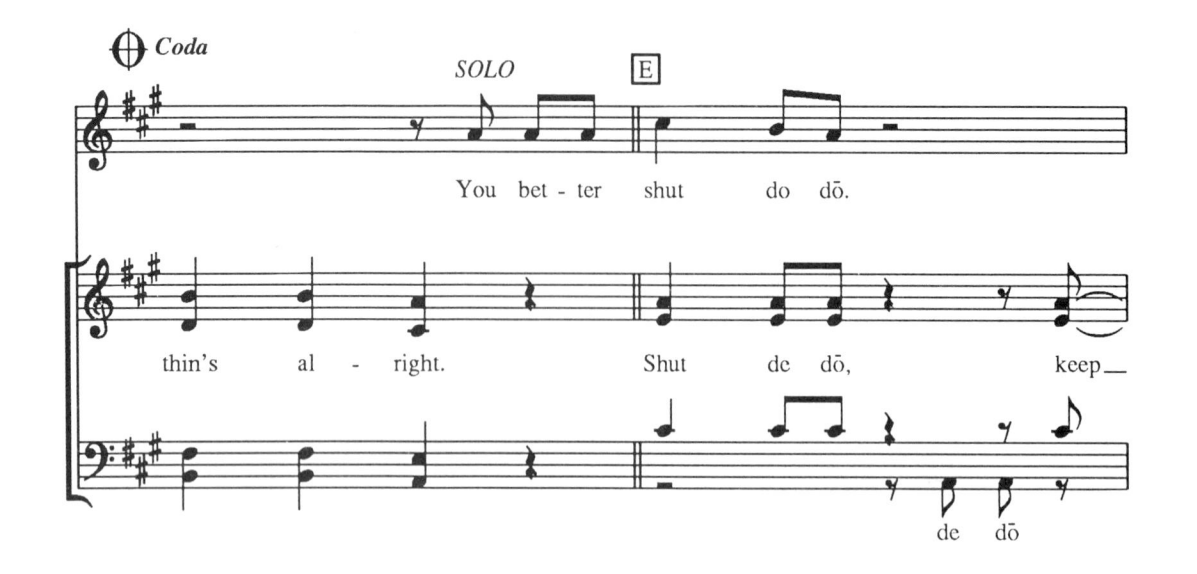

light de can - dle, ev - 'ry - thin's al - right.
Light de can - dle, ev - 'ry - thin's al - right. Light de can - dle, ev - 'ry-
Whoa, Whoo
thin's al - right. Light de can - dle, ev - 'ry - thin's al - right.
(ad lib)
rit.
Ev - 'ry - thin's al - right!
rit.
Light de can - dle, ev - 'ry - thin's al - right!

The River

Words and Music by
Garth Brooks and Victoria Shaw
Arranged by Carl Strommen

SATB, Accompanied with Optional Guitar, Bass, and Drums

dream is like a riv-er ever chang-ing as it flows. And the
times we stand a-side, let the wa-ters slip a-way; What we

*Guitar: Play ad lib. from chord symbols in piano part.
Bass: Double bottom notes in left hand of piano part, adjusting octaves whenever necessary.

Copyright © 1989 MAJOR BOB MUSIC CO., INC. (ASCAP), MID-SUMMER MUSIC CO., INC. (ASCAP) and GARY MORRIS MUSIC
International Copyright Secured   Made in U.S.A.   All Rights Reserved

dream-er's just a ves-sel that must fol-low where it goes. Try-ing to
put off 'til to-mor-row has now be-come to-day. So, don't you

learn from what's be-hind you and nev-er know-ing what's in store makes each
sit up-on the shore-line and say you're sat - is-fied.

day a con-stant bat-tle just to stay be-tween the shores.
Choose to chance the rap-ids and dare to dance the tide.

The River 205

And I will sail my ves-sel 'til the riv-er runs dry. Like a bird up-on the wind, these wa-ters are my sky. I'll nev-er reach my des-ti-na-tion if I nev-er try. I will

206 *Choral Connections Level 3 Mixed Voices*

*Original text: Good Lord.

208 *Choral Connections Level 3 Mixed Voices*

The River

Look-A That Star

Words and Music by
Jay Althouse

SATB Voices, A cappella

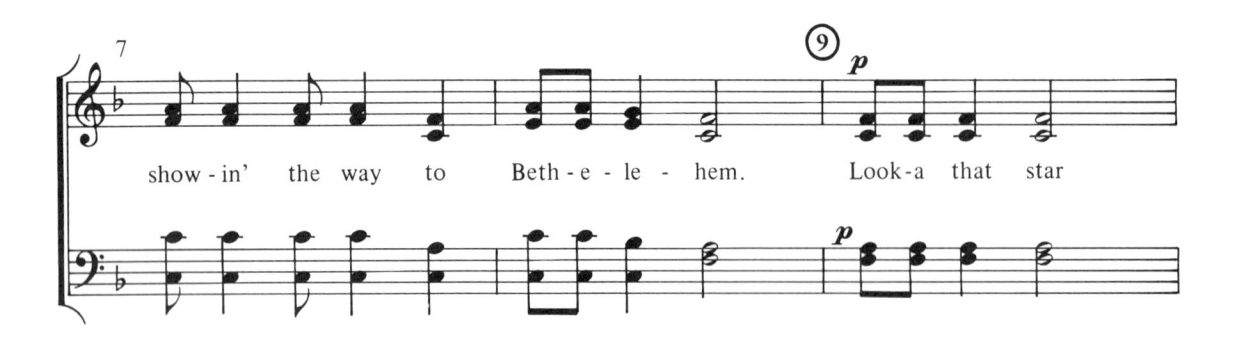

Brightly, in two (𝅗𝅥 = ca. 112-116)

Look-a that star shine in the night. Look-a that star shine in the night. Look-a that star shine in the night, showin' the way to Beth-e-le-hem. Look-a that star

*Also available for 3-part mixed voices (4732).

© Copyright MCMXCII by Alfred Publishing Co., Inc.

10
cresc.
shine in the night. Look-a that star shine in the night. Look-a that star
cresc.
14
f
shine in the night, show-in' the way to Beth-e-le-hem.
f
17
1st VERSE: female solo
f
1. Mar-y and Jo-seph saw that star.
2nd VERSE: male solo
f
2. Mar-y had a lit-tle ba-by boy.
S.
A.
mf
Show-in' the way to
T.
B.
mf

212 Choral Connections Level 3 Mixed Voices

Look-A That Star

214 *Choral Connections   Level 3 Mixed Voices*

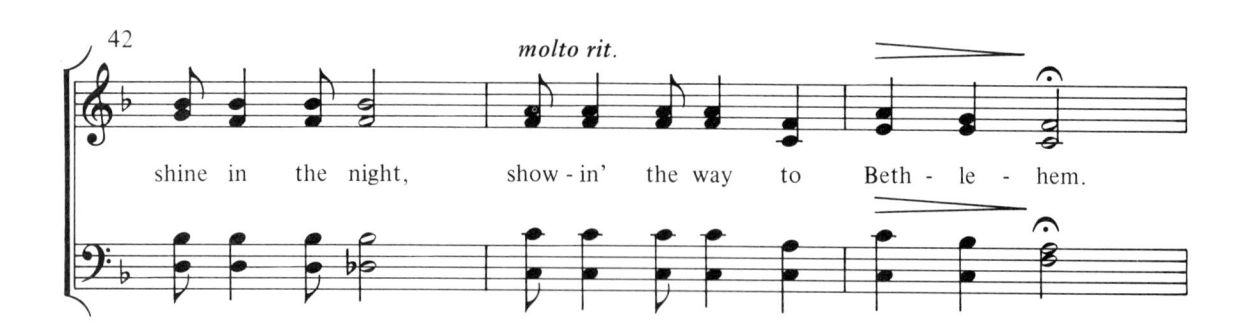

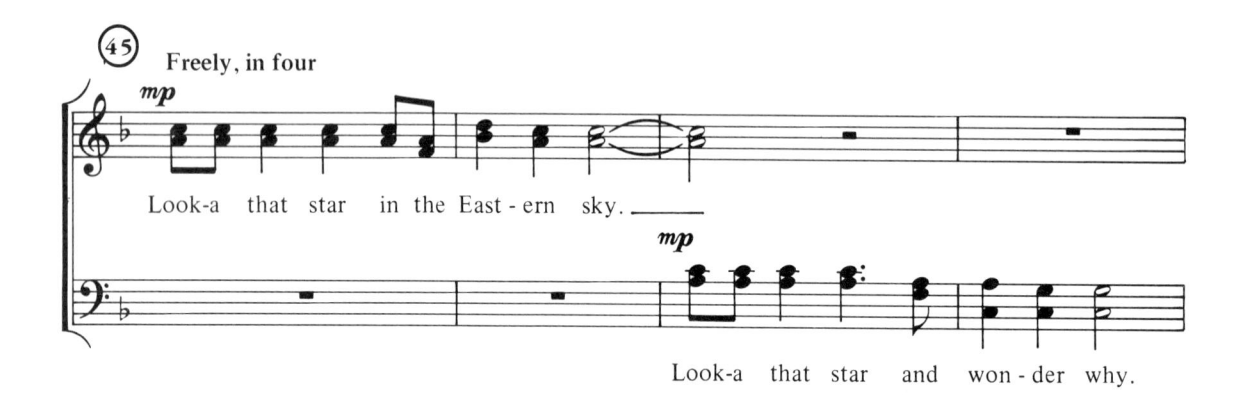

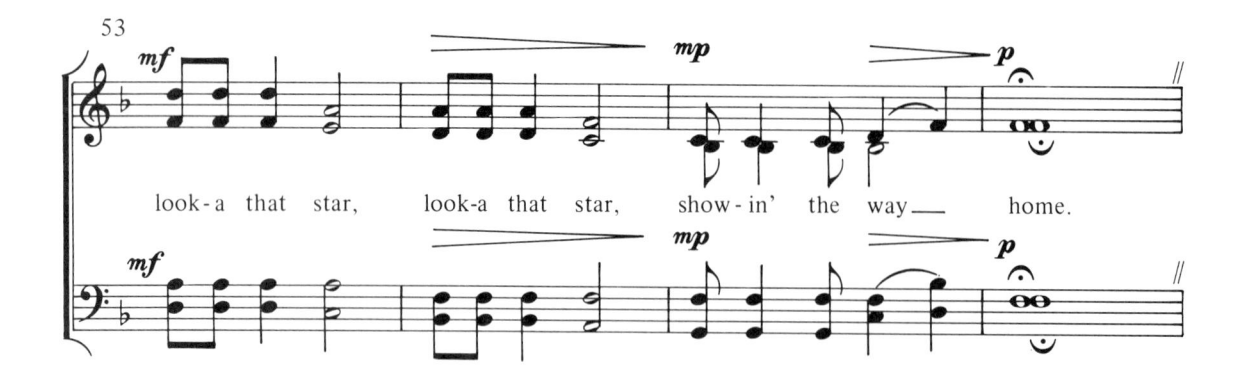

Look-A That Star

216 Choral Connections Level 3 Mixed Voices

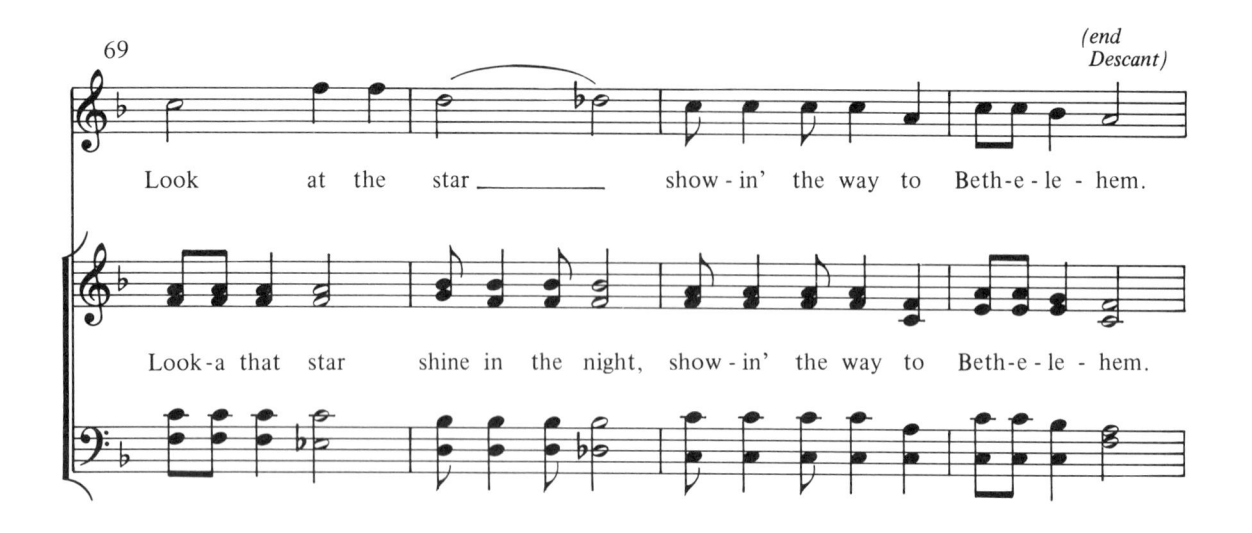

A Holiday Wish

Words and Music by
Jay Althouse

SATB Voices and Piano

Gently (♩ = ca. 92-100)

What I want most of all this Christmas is a

* Also available for S.A.B., Level Three (11313), and 2-part, Level Two (11314).
SoundTrax Cassette available (3896).

Copyright © MCMXCIV by Alfred Publishing Co., Inc.
All rights reserved.   Printed in USA.

A Holiday Wish **217**

world of love and peace, where all ha-tred and fear have end-ed and war shall ev-er cease. In this ver-y spe-cial sea-son of pleas-ures great and small, we sing of hope and prom-ise and of peace, good-will to all. What I want most of all this Christ-mas is a world where all are free, with a great mul-ti-tude of

A Holiday Wish

27
col - ors who live in har - mo - ny.
30
mp unis.
In this
34
cresc.
ver - y spe - cial sea - son of pleas - ures great and
unis. mp
oo
oo
oo
cresc.

A Holiday Wish

222 *Choral Connections Level 3 Mixed Voices*

For the Mark Twain J.H.S. Chorus and
The Western Wind Vocal Ensemble
Commissioned by "Meet the Composer"

El Progreso Honduras

Elliot Z. Levine
Sheila Maldonado

Two-part Mixed Choruses (SAB and SATB) A cappella

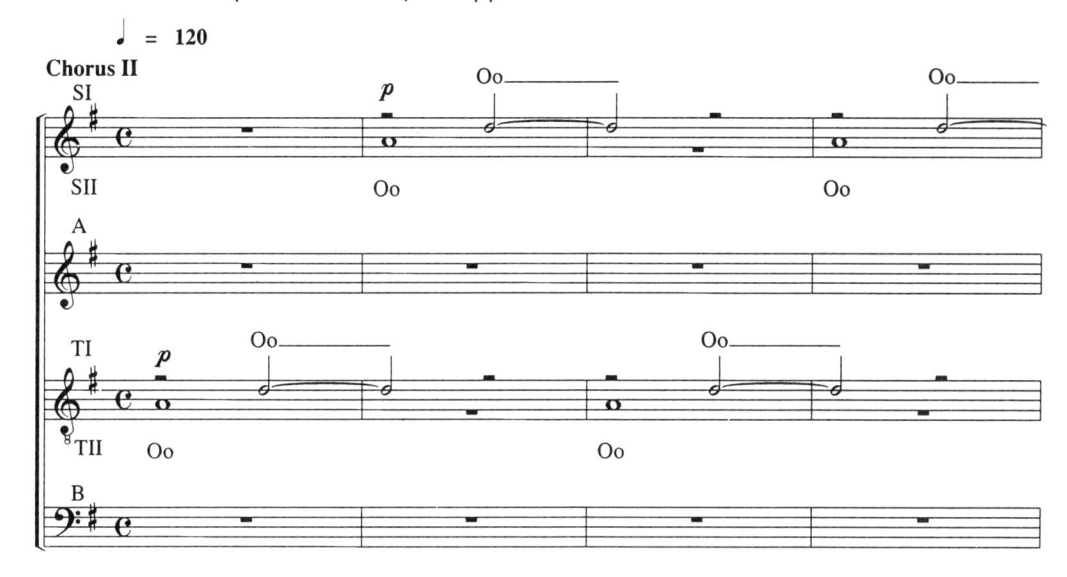

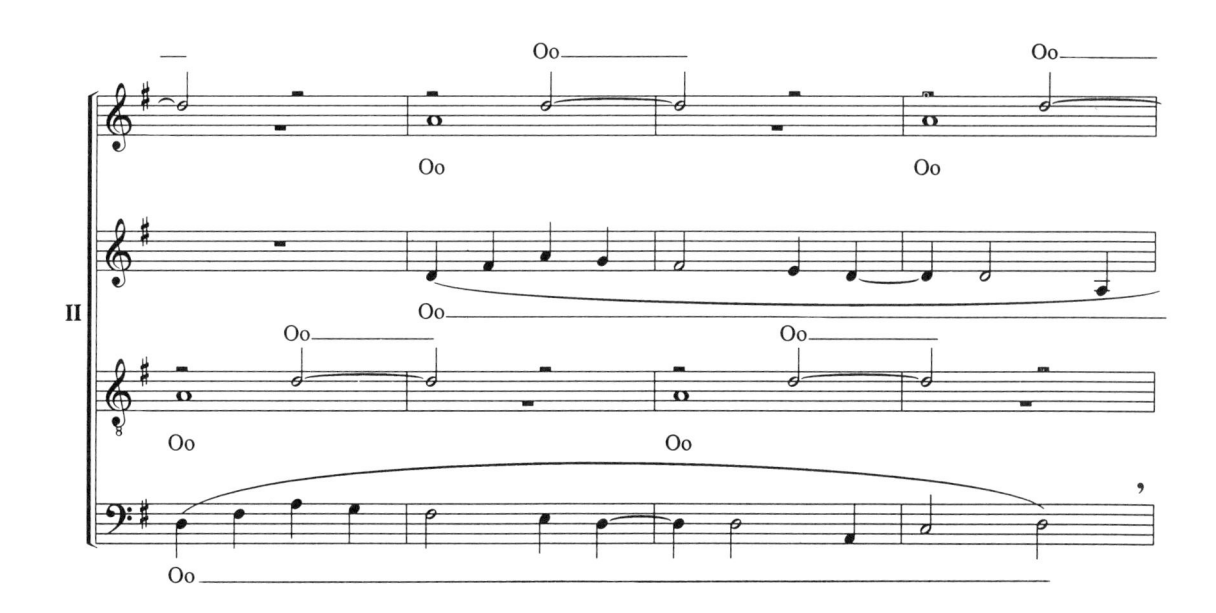

♩ = 120

Copyright © 1994 Plymouth Music Co., Inc., 170 N.E. 33rd St., Ft. Lauderdale, FL 33334
International Copyright Secured   Made in U.S.A.   All Rights Reserved

Chorus I
S
mf
11
Sobre las montañas vimos las nubes y nosotros nos prepa-
A
mf
Sobre las montañas vimos las nubes y nosotros nos prepa-
B
mf
Sobre las montañas vimos las nubes y nosotros nos prepa-
Chorus II
Oo
Oo
Oo
Oo
Oo
Oo
Oo
Oo
ramos para la lluvia.
SI
SII
f
Above the
I
ramos para la lluvia.
f
Above the
ramos para la lluvia.
Oo
Oo
Oo
Oo
Oo
II
Oo
tacet
Oo
Oo

El Progreso Honduras

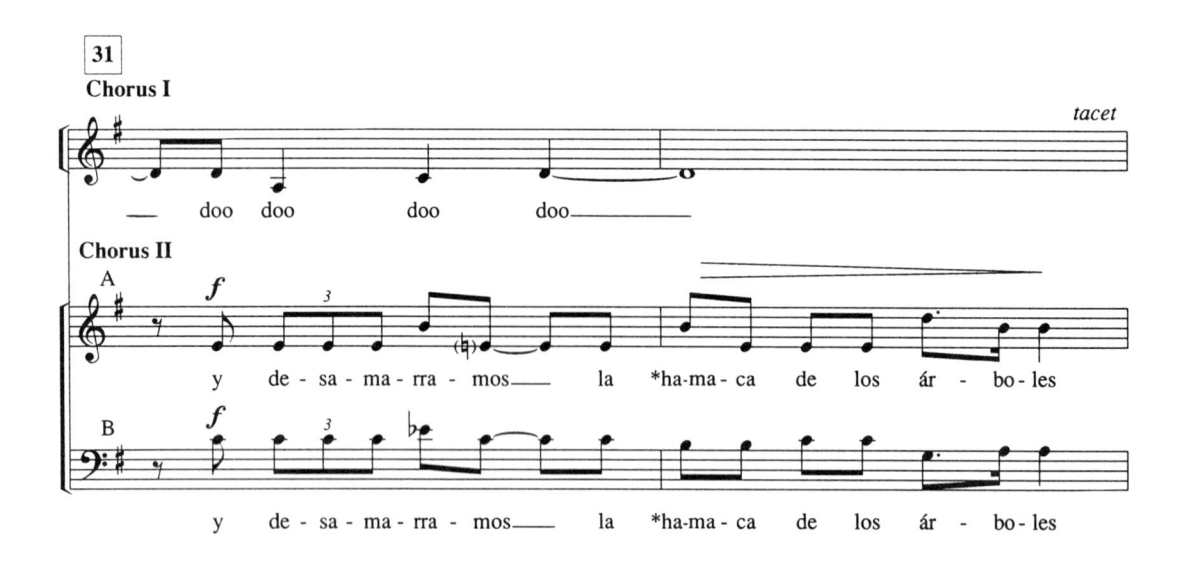

*Pronounced mah-kah

El Progreso Honduras

42
Chorus I
S
legato
p
lor del dí - a
Ju -
A
p
lor del dí - a
Ju -
B
p
lor del dí - a
Ju -
Chorus II
A
p
3
tacet
doo doo doo doo doo doo doo doo doo doo doo doo doo doo
B
p
3
tacet
doo doo doo doo doo doo doo doo doo doo doo doo doo doo

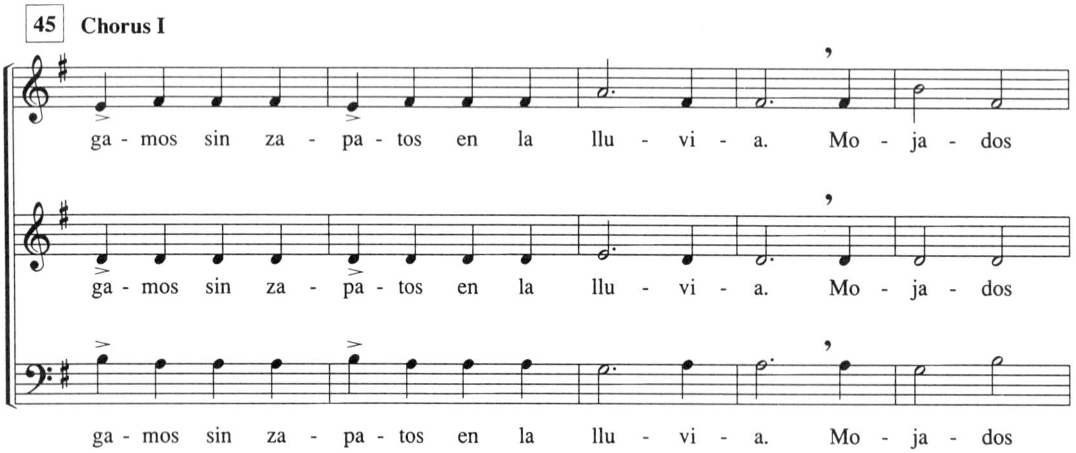
45
Chorus I
ga - mos sin za - pa - tos en la llu - vi - a. Mo - ja - dos
ga - mos sin za - pa - tos en la llu - vi - a. Mo - ja - dos
ga - mos sin za - pa - tos en la llu - vi - a. Mo - ja - dos

El Progreso Honduras

Sing 4 times - pp, mp, mf, whisper (no pitch)
58
SA
pp
I
Sobre las montañas vimos las nubes
B
pp
Sobre las montañas vimos las nubes
SA
II
tañas vimos las nubes y nosotros
TB
mos las nubes y nosotros nos prepa-
60
Fine
y nosotros nos preparamos para la lluvia
Fine
y nosotros nos preparamos para la lluvia
Fine
mp
nos preparamos para la lluvia
Sobre las mon-
Fine
mp
ramos para la lluvia
Sobre las montañas vi-

Glossary

Choral Music Terms

A

a cappella (ah-kah-PEH-lah) [It.] Unaccompanied vocal music.

accelerando (*accel.*) (ah-chel-leh-RAHN-doh) [It.] Gradually increasing the tempo.

accent Indicates the note is to be sung with extra force or stress. (>)

accidentals Signs used to indicate the raising or lowering of a pitch. A sharp (#) alters a pitch by raising it one-half step; a flat (♭) alters a pitch by lowering it one-half step; a natural (♮) cancels a sharp or a flat.

accompaniment Musical material that supports another; for example, a piano or orchestra accompanying a choir or soloist.

adagio (ah-DAH-jee-oh) [It.] Slow tempo, but not as slow as largo.

ad libitum (ad. lib.) [Lt.] An indication that the performer may vary the tempo, add or delete a vocal or instrumental part. Synonymous with a *piacere*.

al fine (ahl FEE-neh) [It.] To the end.

alla breve Indicates cut time; duple meter in which there are two beats per measure, the half note getting one beat. (¢)

allargando (*allarg.*) (ahl-ahr-GAHN-doh) [It.] To broaden, become slower.

aleatoric or chance music Music in which chance is deliberately used as a compositional component.

allegro (ah-LEH-groh) [It.] Brisk tempo; faster than moderato, slower than *vivace*.

allegro assai (ah-LEH-groh ah-SAH-ee) [It.] Very fast; in seventeenth-century music, the term can also mean "sufficiently fast."

altered pitch A note that does not belong to the scale of the work being performed.

alto The lower female voice; sometimes called contralto or mezzo-soprano.

anacrusis (a-nuh-KROO-suhs) [Gk.] *See* upbeat.

andante (ahn-DAHN-teh) [It.] Moderately slow; a walking tempo.

andante con moto (ahn-DAHN-teh kohn MOH-toh) [It.] A slightly faster tempo, "with motion."

animato Quick, lively; "animated."

anthem A choral composition in English using a sacred text. *See also* motet.

antiphonal Music performed by alternating ensembles, positioned in opposing locations, as in choirs or brass; first brought to prominence by Giovanni Gabrielli at St. Mark's Cathedral, Venice, in the Baroque period.

appassionato (uh-pah-shun-NAHT-oh) [It.] With deep feeling, passionately.

appoggiatura (uh-pah-zhuh-TOOR-uh) [It.] A nonharmonic tone, usually a half or whole step above the harmonic tone, performed on the beat, resolving downward to the harmonic tone.

aria (AHR-ee-uh) [It.] A song for a solo singer and orchestra, usually in an opera, oratorio, or cantata.

arpeggio (ahr-PEH-jee-oh) [It.] A chord in which the pitches are sounded successively, usually from lowest to highest; in broken style.

art song Expressive songs about life, love, and human relationships for solo voice and piano.

articulation Clarity in performance of notes and diction.

a tempo (ah TEM-poh) [It.] Return to the established tempo after a change.

atonality Music not organized around a key center.

augmentation A technique used in composition by which the melody line is repeated in doubled note values; opposite of *diminution*.

augmented The term indicating that a major or perfect interval has been enlarged by one-half step; as in C-F# (augmented fourth) or C-G# (augmented fifth).

B

balance and symmetry Even and equal.

baritone The male voice between tenor and bass.

bar line (measure bar) A vertical line drawn through the staff to show the end of a measure. Double bar lines show the end of a section or a piece of music.

Bar Line   Double Bar Line

Baroque period (buh-ROHK) [Fr.] Historic period between c. 1600 and c. 1750 that reflected highly embellished styles in art, architecture, fashion, manners, and music. The period of elaboration.

bass The lowest male voice, below tenor and baritone.

bass clef Symbol at the beginning of the staff for lower voices and instruments, or the piano left hand; usually referring to pitches lower than middle C. The two dots lie on either side of the fourth-line F, thus the term, F clef.

beat A steady pulse.

bel canto (bell KAHN-toh) [It.] Italian vocal technique of the eighteenth century with emphasis on beauty of sound and brilliance of performance.

binary form Defines a form having two sections (A and B), each of which may be repeated.

bitonality The designation of music written in two different keys at the same time.

breath mark A mark placed within a phrase or melody showing where the singer or musician should breathe. (')

C

cadence Punctuation or termination of a musical phrase; a breathing break.

caesura (si-ZHUR-uh) [Lt.] A break or pause between two musical phrases. (//)

call and response A song style that follows a simple question-and-answer pattern in which a soloist leads and a group responds.

calypso style Folk-style music from the Caribbean Islands with bright, syncopated rhythm.

cambiata The young male voice that is still developing.

canon A compositional form in which the subject is begun in one group and then is continually and exactly repeated by other groups. Unlike the round, the canon closes with all voices ending together on a common chord.

cantata (kan-TAH-tuh) [It.] A collection of vocal compositions with instrumental accompaniment consisting of several movements based on related secular or sacred text segments.

cantabile In a lyrical, singing style.

cantor A solo singer in the Jewish and Roman Catholic traditions who leads the congregation in worship by introducing responses and other musical portions of the services.

cantus firmus (KAHN-tuhs FUHR-muhs) [Lt.] A previously-composed melody which is used as a basis for a new composition.

chance music See aleatoric music.

chantey (SHAN-tee) [Fr.] A song sung by sailors in rhythm with their work.

chant, plainsong Music from the liturgy of the early church, characterized by free rhythms, monophonic texture, and sung *a cappella*.

chorale (kuh-RAL) [Gr.] Congregational song or hymn of the German Protestant (Evangelical) Church.

chord Three or more pitches sounded simultaneously.

chord, block Three or more pitches sounded simultaneously.

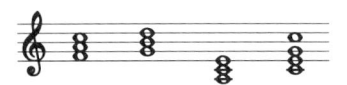

chord, broken Three or more pitches sounded in succession; *see also* arpeggio.

chromatic (kroh-MAT-ik) [Gr.] Moving up or down by half steps. Also the name of a scale composed entirely of half steps.

Classical period The period in Western history beginning around 1750 and lasting until around 1820 that reflected a time when society began looking to the ancient Greeks and Romans for examples of order and ways of looking at life.

clef The symbol at the beginning of the staff that identifies a set of pitches; *see also* bass clef and treble clef.

coda Ending section; a concluding portion of a composition. (⊕)

common time Another name for 4/4 meter; *see also* cut time. (**c**)

composer The creator of musical works.

compound meter Meter whose beat can be subdivided into threes and/or sixes.

con (kohn) [It.] With.

con brio (kohn BREE-oh) [It.] With spirit; vigorously.

concerto Composition for solo instrument and an orchestra, usually with three movements.

con moto (kohn MOH-toh) [It.] With motion.

consonance A musical interval or chord that sounds pleasing; opposite of dissonance.

Contemporary period The time from 1900 to right now.

continuo A Baroque tradition in which the bass line is played "continuously," by a cello, double bass, and/or bassoon while a keyboard instrument (harpsichord, organ) plays the bass line and indicated harmonies.

contrapuntal See counterpoint.

counterpoint The combination of simultaneous parts; *see* polyphony.

crescendo (*cresc.*) (kreh-SHEN-doh) [It.] To gradually become louder.

cued notes Smaller notes indicating either optional harmony or notes from another voice part.

cut time 2/2 time with the half note getting the beat. (¢)

D

da capo (*D.C.*) (dah KAH-poh) [It.] Go back to the beginning and repeat; *see also* dal segno and al fine.

dal segno (*D.S.*) (dahl SAYN-yoh) [It.] Go back to the sign and repeat. (𝄋)

D. C. al fine (dah KAH-poh ahl FEE-neh) [It.] Repeat back to the beginning and end at the "fine."

decrescendo (*decresc.*) (deh-kreh-SHEN-doh) [It.] To gradually become softer.

delicato Delicate; to play or sing delicately.

descant A high, ornamental voice part often lying above the melody.

diaphragm The muscle that separates the chest cavity (thorax) from the abdomen. The primary muscle in the inhalation/exhalation cycle.

diction Clear and correct enunciation.

diminished The term describing an interval that has been descreased by half steps; for example, the *perfect fourth* (3 whole and one half steps) becomes a *diminished fourth* (3 whole steps). Also used for a triad which has a minor third (R, 3) and a diminished fifth (R, 5); for example, C, E♭, G♭.

diminuendo (*dim.*) (duh-min-yoo-WEN-doh) [It.] Gradually getting softer; *see also* decrescendo.

diminution The halving of values; that is, halves become quarters, quarters become eighths, etc. Opposite of *augmentation*.

diphthong A combination of two vowel sounds consisting of a primary vowel sound and a secondary vowel sound. The secondary vowel sound is (usually) at the very end of the diphthong; for example, in the word *toy*, the diphthong starts with the sound of "o," then moves on to "y," in this case pronounced "ee."

dissonance Discord in music, suggesting a state of tension or "seeking"; chords using seconds, fourths, fifths, and sevenths; the opposite of consonance.

divisi (*div.*) (dih-VEE-see) [It.] Divide; the parts divide.

dolce (DOHL-chay) [It.] Sweet; *dolcissimo*, very sweet; *dolcemente*, sweetly.

dominant The fifth degree of a major or minor scale; the triad built on the fifth degree; indicated as V in harmonic analysis.

Dorian mode A scale with the pattern of whole-step, half, whole, whole, whole, half, and whole. For example, D to D on the keyboard.

dotted rhythm A note written with a dot increases its value again by half.

double bar Two vertical lines placed on the staff indicating the end of a section or a composition; used with two dots to enclose repeated sections.

double flat (♭♭) Symbol showing the lowering of a pitch one whole step (two half steps).

double sharp (𝄪) Symbol showing the raising of a pitch one whole step (two half steps).

doubling The performance of the same note by two parts, either at the same pitch or an octave apart.

downbeat The accented first beat in a measure.

D. S. al coda (dahl SAYN-yoh ahl KOH-dah) [It.] Repeat from the symbol (𝄋) and skip to the coda when you see the sign. (⊕)

D. S. al fine (dahl SAYN-yoh ahl FEE-neh) [It.] Repeat from the symbol (𝄋) and sing to fine or the end.

duple Any time signature or group of beats that is a multiple of two.

duet Composition for two performers.

dynamics The volume of sound, the loudness or softness of a musical passage; intensity, power.

E

enharmonic Identical tones that are named and written differently; for example, C sharp and D flat.

ensemble A group of musicians or singers who perform together.

enunciation Speaking and singing words with distinct vowels and consonants.

espressivo (*espress.*) (es-preh-SEE-vo) [It.] For expression; *con espressione*, with feeling.

ethnomusicology The musical study of specific world cultures.

expressive singing To sing with feeling.

exuberance Joyously unrestrained and enthusiastic.

F

fermata (fur-MAH-tah) [It.] A hold; to hold the note longer. (𝄐)

fine (FEE-neh) Ending; to finish.

flat Symbol (accidental) that lowers a pitch by one half step. (♭)

folk music Uncomplicated music that speaks directly of everyday matters; the first popular music; usually passed down through the oral tradition.

form The structure of a musical composition.

forte (*f*) (FOR-teh) [It.] Loud.

fortissimo (*ff*) (for-TEE-suh-moh) [It.] Very loud.

freely A direction that permits liberties with tempo, dynamics, and style.

fugue (FYOOG) [It.] A polyphonic composition consisting of a series of successive melody imitations; *see also* imitative style.

fusion A combination or blending of different genres of music.

G

gapped scale A scale resulting from leaving out certain tones (the pentatonic scale is an example).

grandioso [It.] Stately, majestic.

grand staff Two staves usually linked together by a long bar line and a bracket.

grave (GRAH-veh) [It.] Slow, solemn.

grazioso (grah-tsee-OH-soh) [It.] Graceful.

H

half step The smallest distance (interval) between two notes on a keyboard; the chromatic scale is composed entirely of half steps, shown as (v).

half time *See* cut time.

harmonic interval Intervals that are sung or played simultaneously; *see also* melodic interval.

harmony Vertical blocks of different tones sounded simultaneously.

hemiola (hee-mee-OH-lah) [Gk.] A metric flow of two against a metric flow of three.

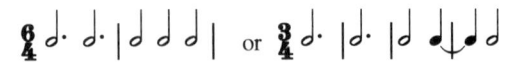

homophonic (hah-muh-FAH-nik) [Gk.] A texture where all parts sing similar rhythm in unison or harmony.

homophony (hah-MAH-fuh-nee) [Gk.] Music that consists of two or more voice parts with similar or identical rhythms. From the Greek words meaning "same sounds," homophony could be described as "hymn-style."

hushed A style marking indicating a soft, whispered tone.

I

imitation, imitative style Restating identical or nearly identical musical material in two or more parts.

improvised Invented on the spur of the moment.

improvisation Spontaneous musical invention, commonly associated with jazz.

interval The distance from one note to another; intervals are measured by the total steps and half steps between the two notes.

intonation The degree to which pitch is accurately produced in tune.

introduction An opening section at the beginning of a movement or work, preparatory to the main body of the form.

inversion May be applied to melody and harmony: *melodic inversion* occurs in an exchange of ascending and descending movement (for instance, a third becomes a sixth, a fourth becomes a fifth, etc.); *harmonic inversion* occurs in the position of the chord tones (that is, root position with the root as lowest tone, first inversion with the third as lowest tone, and second inversion with the fifth as the lowest tone).

K

key The way tonality is organized around a tonal center; *see also* key signature.

key change Changing an initial key signature in the body of a composition.

key signature Designation of sharps or flats at the beginning of a composition to indicate its basic scale and tonality.

L

leading tone The seventh degree of a scale, so called because of its strong tendency to resolve upward to the tonic.

legato (leh-GAH-toh) [It.] Smooth, connected style.

ledger lines Short lines that appear above, between treble and bass clefs, or below the bass clef, used to expand the notation.

leggiero (leh-JEH-roh) [It.] Articulate lightly; sometimes nonlegato.

lento Slow; a little faster than *largo*, a little slower than *adagio*.

linear flow, line Singing/playing notes in a flowing (smooth) manner, as if in a horizontal line.

liturgical Pertaining to prescribed forms of worship or ritual in various religious services. Western music contains much literature written for the liturgy of the early Roman Catholic Church.

lullaby A cradle song; in Western music, usually sung with a gentle and regular rhythm.

M

madrigal A secular vocal form in several parts, popular in the Renaissance.

maestoso (mah-eh-STOH-soh) [It.] Perform majestically.

major (key, scale, mode) Scale built on the formula of two whole steps, one half step, three whole steps, one half step.

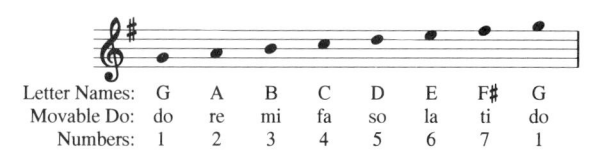

Letter Names:	G	A	B	C	D	E	F#	G
Movable Do:	do	re	mi	fa	so	la	ti	do
Numbers:	1	2	3	4	5	6	7	1

Major 2nd The name for an interval of one whole step or two half steps. For example, from C to D.

Major 6th The name for an interval of four whole steps and one-half step. For example, from C to A.

Major 3rd The name for an interval of two whole steps or four half steps. For example, from C to E.

major triad Three tones that form a major third *do* to *mi* and a minor third *mi* to *so* as in C E G.

marcato (mahr-KAH-toh) [It.] Long but separated pitches; translated as marked.

mass The main religious service of the Roman Catholic Church. There are two divisions of mass: the Proper of the Mass in which the text changes for each day, and the Ordinary of the Mass in which the text remains the same for every mass. Music for the mass includes the Kyrie, Gloria, Credo, Sanctus, and Agnus Dei as well as other chants, hymns, and psalms. For special mass occasions composers through the centuries have created large musical works for choruses, soloists, instrumentalists, and orchestras.

measure The space from one bar line to the next; also called bars.

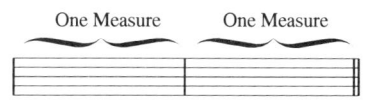

medieval Historical period prior to the Renaissance, c. 500-1450.

medley A group of tunes, linked together and sung consecutively.

melisma (n.) or melismatic (adj.) (muh-LIZ-mah or muh-liz-MAT-ik) [Gk.] A term describing the setting of one syllable of text to several pitches.

melodic interval Intervals that are performed in succession; *see also* harmonic interval.

melody A logical succession of musical tones; also called tune.

meter The pattern into which a steady succession of rhythmic pulses (beats) is organized.

meter signature The divided number at the beginning of a clef; 4/4, 3/4, and so forth; *see also* time signature.

metronome marking A sign that appears over the top line of the treble clef staff at the beginning of a piece indicating the tempo. It shows the kind of note that will get the beat and the numbers of beats per minute as measured by a metronome; for example, ♪ = 100.

mezzo forte (*mf*) (MEHT-soh FOR-teh) [It.] Medium loud.

mezzo piano (*mp*) (MEHT-soh pee-AH-noh) [It.] Medium soft.

mezzo voce (MET-soh VOH-cheh) [It.] With half voice; reduced volume and tone.

middle C The note that is located nearest the center of the piano keyboard; middle C can be written in either the treble or bass clef.

minor (key, scale) Scale built on the formula of one whole step, one half step, two whole steps, one half step, two whole steps.

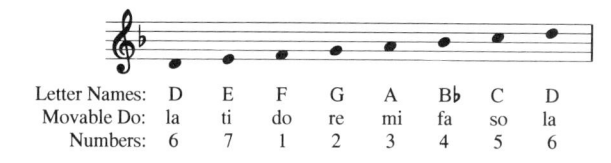

Letter Names:	D	E	F	G	A	B♭	C	D
Movable Do:	la	ti	do	re	mi	fa	so	la
Numbers:	6	7	1	2	3	4	5	6

minor mode One of two modes upon which the basic scales of Western music are based, the other being major; using W for a whole step and H for a half step, a minor scale has the pattern W H W W H W W.

minor triad Three tones that form a minor third (bottom) and a major third (top), such as A C E.

minor third The name for an interval of three half steps. For example, from A to C.

mixed meter Frequently changing time signatures or meters.

moderato Moderate.

modulation Adjusting to a change of keys within a song.

molto Very or much; for example, *molto rit.* means "much slower."

monophonic (mah-nuh-FAH-nik) [Gk.] A musical texture having a single melodic line with no accompaniment; monophony.

monophony (muh-NAH-fuh-nee) [Gk.] One sound; music that has a single melody. Gregorian chants or plainsongs exhibit monophony.

motet Originating as a Medieval and Renaissance polyphonic song, this choral form of composition became an unaccompanied work, often in contrapuntal style.

motive A shortened expression, sometimes contained within a phrase.

musical variations Changes in rhythm, pitch, dynamics, style, and tempo to create new statements of the established theme.

mysterioso Perform in a mysterious or haunting way; to create a haunting mood.

N

nationalism Patriotism; pride of country. This feeling influenced many Romantic composers such as Wagner, Tchaikovsky, Dvořák, Chopin, and Brahms.

natural (♮) Cancels a previous sharp (♯) lowering the pitch a half step, or a previous flat (♭), raising the pitch a half step.

no breath mark A direction not to take a breath at a specific place in the composition. (♩♩ or N.B.)

non-harmonic tones Identifies those pitches outside the harmonic structure of the chord; for example, the *passing tone* and the *appoggiatura*.

non troppo (nahn TROH-poh) [It.] Not too much; for example, allegro non troppo, not too fast.

notation Written notes, symbols, and directions used to represent music within a composition.

nuance Subtle variations in tempo, phrasing, dynamics, etc., to enhance the musical performance.

O

octave An interval of twelve half steps; 8 or 8va = an octave above; 8vb = an octave below.

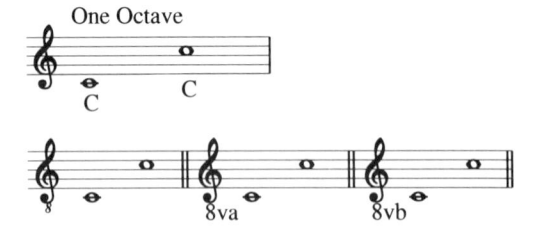

opera A combination of singing, instrumental music, dancing, and drama that tells a story.

operetta A lighter, "popular" style of operatic form, including sung and spoken dialogue, solo, chorus, and dance.

optional divisi (*opt. div.*) Indicating a split in the music into optional harmony, shown by the smaller cued note.

opus, Op. The term, meaning "work," used by composers to show the chronological order of their works; for example, Opus 1, Op. 2.

oratorio A piece for solo voices, chorus, and orchestra, that is an expanded dramatic work on a literary or religious theme presented without theatrical action.

ostinato (ahs-tuh-NAH-toh) [It.] A rhythmic or melodic passage that is repeated continuously.

overtones The almost inaudible higher pitches which occur over the fundamental tone, resulting from the division of the vibrating cycle into smaller segments; compare to partials, harmonics.

P

palate The roof of the mouth; the *hard palate* is forward, the *soft palate* (*velum*) is at the back.

parallel major and minor keys Major and minor keys having the same tonic, such as A major and A minor (A major being the parallel major of A minor and A minor the parallel minor of A major).

parallel motion The movement of two or more voice parts in the same direction, at the same interval from each other.

peak The high point in the course of a development; for example, the high point of a musical phrase or the high point in a movement of instrumental music.

pentatonic scale A five-tone scale constructed of *do, re, mi, so, la* (degrees 1, 2, 3, 5, 6) of a corresponding major scale.

Perfect 5th The name for an interval of three whole steps and one half step. For example, C to G.

Perfect 4th The name for an interval of two whole steps and one half step. For example, C to F.

phrase A musical sentence containing a beginning, middle, and end.

phrase mark In music, an indicator of the length of a phrase in a melody; this mark may also mean that the singer or musician should not take a breath for the duration of the phrase. (⌢)

phrasing The realization of the phrase structure of a work; largely a function of a performer's articulation and breathing.

pianissimo (*pp*) (pee-uh-NEE-suh-moh) [It.] Very soft.

piano (*p*) (pee-ANN-noh) [It.] Soft.

Picardy third An interval of a major third used in the final, tonic chord of a piece written in a minor key.

pick-up *See* upbeat.

pitch Sound, the result of vibration; the highness or lowness of a tone, determined by the number of vibrations per second.

piu (pew) [It.] More; for example, *piu forte* means "more loudly."

poco (POH-koh) [It.] Little; for example, *poco dim.* means "a little softer."

poco a poco (POH-koh ah POH-koh) [It.] Little by little; for example, *poco a poco cresc.* means "little by little increase in volume."

polyphony (n.) or polyphonic (adj.) (pah-LIH-fuh-nee or pah-lee-FAH-nik) [Gk.] The term that means that each voice part begins at a different place, is independent and important, and that sections often repeat in contrasting dynamic levels. Poly = many, phony = sounds.

polyrhythmic The simultaneous use of contrasting rhythmic figures.

presto (PREH-stoh) [It.] Very fast.

program music A descriptive style of music composed to relate or illustrate a specific incident, situation, or drama; the form of the piece is often dictated or influenced by the nonmusical program. This style commonly occurs in music composed during the Romantic period. For example, "The Moldau" from *Má Vlast*, by Bedrich Smetana.

progression A succession of two or more pitches or chords; also melodic or harmonic progression.

R

rallentando (*rall.*) (rahl-en-TAHN-doh) [It.] Meaning to "perform more and more slowly." *See also* ritardando.

recitative (res-uh-TAY-teev) [It.] A speechlike style of singing used in opera, oratorio, and cantata.

register, vocal A term used for different parts of a singer's range, such as head register (high notes) and chest register (low notes).

relative major and minor keys The relative minor of any major key or scale, while sharing its key signature and pitches, takes for its tonic the sixth scale degree of that major key or scale. For example, in D major the sixth scale degree is B (or *la* in solfège), *la* then becomes the tonic for B minor.

D major   B minor

Renaissance period The historic period in Western Europe from c. 1430 to 1600; the term means "rebirth" or "renewal"; it indicates a period of rapid development in exploration, science, art, and music.

repeat sign A direction to repeat the section of music (‖:‖); if the first half of this sign is omitted, it means to "go back to the beginning" (:‖).

repetition The restatement of a musical idea; repeated pitches; repeated "A" section in ABA form.

resolution (*res.*) A progression from a dissonant tone or harmony to a consonant harmony; a sense of completion.

resonance Reinforcement and intensification of sound by vibrations.

rest Symbols used to indicated silence.

rhythm The pattern of sounds and silences.

rhythmic motif A rhythmic pattern that is repeated throughout a movement or composition.

ritardando (*rit.*) The gradual slowing of tempo; also called "ritard."

Rococo Music of the Baroque period so elaborate it was named after a certain type of fancy rock work.

Romantic period A historic period starting c. 1820 and ending c. 1900 in which artists and composers attempted to break with classical music ideas.

rondo form An instrumental form based on an alternation between a repeated (or recurring) section and contrasting episodes (ABACADA).

root The bottom note of a triad in its original position; the note on which the chord is built.

round A composition in which the perpetual theme (sometimes with harmonic parts) begins in one group and is strictly imitated in other groups in an overlapping fashion. Usually the last voice to enter becomes the final voice to complete the song.

rubato (roo-BAH-toh) [It.] Freely; allows the conductor or the performer to vary the tempo.

S

sacred music Of or dealing with religious music; hymns, chorales, early masses; *see* secular music.

scale A pattern of pitches arranged by whole steps and half steps.

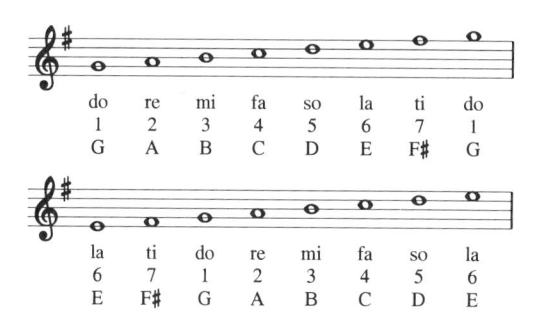

do	re	mi	fa	so	la	ti	do
1	2	3	4	5	6	7	1
G	A	B	C	D	E	F#	G

la	ti	do	re	mi	fa	so	la
6	7	1	2	3	4	5	6
E	F#	G	A	B	C	D	E

score The arrangement of instrumental and vocal staffs that all sound at the same time.

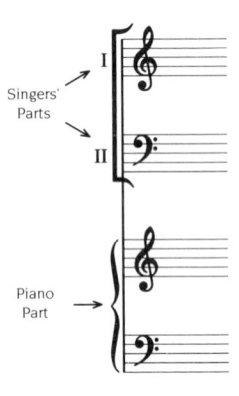

secular music Music without religious content; *see* sacred music.

sempre (SEHM-preh) [It.] Always, continually.

seventh chord By adding a seventh above the root of a triad (R, 3, 5), the result is a four-tone chord (R, 3, 5, 7).

sforzando (*sfz*) (sfohr-TSAHN-doh) [It.] A sudden strong accent on a note or chord.

sharp A symbol (accidental) that raises a pitch by one half step. (♯)

sight-sing Reading and singing of music at first sight.

simile (*sim.*) (SIM-ee-leh) [It.] To continue in the same way.

simple meter Meter in which each beat is divisible by 2.

skip Melodic movement in intervals larger than a whole step.

slur Curved line placed over or under a group of notes to indicate that they are to be performed without a break.

solfège (SOHL-fehj) [Fr.] A method of sight-singing, using the syllables *do, re, mi, fa, so, la, ti,* etc. for pitches of the scale.

solo Composition for one featured performer.

sonata-allegro form (suh-NAH-tuh ah-LEH-groh) [It.] Large A B A form consisting of three sections: exposition, development, and recapitulation.

soprano The higher female voice.

sostenuto (SAHS-tuh-noot-oh) [It.] The sustaining of a tone or the slackening of tempo; the right pedal of a piano, which, when depressed, allows the strings to vibrate.

sotto voce In a quiet, subdued manner; "under" the voice.

spirito (SPEE-ree-toh) [It.] Spirited; for example, *con spirito*, with spirit.

spiritual A type of song created by African Americans who combined African rhythms with melodies they created and heard in America.

staccato (stah-KAH-toh) [It.] Performed in a short, detached manner, as opposed to legato.

staff Series of five horizontal lines and four spaces on which music is written to show pitch.

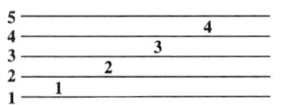

staggered entrances Voice parts or instruments begin singing or playing at different points within the composition.

steady beat A metrical pulse; *see also* beat, meter, rhythm.

step Melodic movement from one note to the next adjacent note, either higher or lower.

stepwise melodic movement Motion from one note to an adjacent one.

stress Emphasis on certain notes or rhythmic elements.

strong beat Naturally accented beats; beats 1 and 3 in 4/4 meter, beat 1 in 3/4 meter.

strophic Description of a song in which all the stanzas of the text are sung to the same music; opposite of *through-composed*.

style The particular character of a musical work; often indicated by words at the beginning of a composition, telling the performer the general manner in which the piece is to be performed.

subito (sub.) (SOO-bee-toh) [It.] Suddenly; for example, *sub. piano* means "suddenly soft."

suspension or suspended tone The tone or tones in a chord that are held as the remainder of the notes change to a new chord. The sustained tones often form a *dissonance* with the new chord, into which they then resolve.

sustained tone A tone sustained in duration; sometimes implying a slowing of tempo; *sostenuto* or *sostenendo*, abbreviated *sost*.

swing This is a performance style in which a pair of eighth notes are no longer performed evenly, but instead like a triplet, yet they are still written; usually indicated at the beginning of a song or a section.

symphony An extended work in several movements, for orchestra; also an orchestra configured to perform symphonic music.

syncopation Deliberate shifts of accent so that a rhythm goes against the steady beat; sometimes referred to as the "offbeat."

240 *Choral Connections*

T

tactus (TAKT-us) [Lt.] The musical term for "beat" in the fifteenth and sixteenth century; generally related to the speed of the human heart.

tempo A pace with which music moves, based on the speed of the underlying beat.

tempo I or tempo primo Return to the first tempo.

tenor A high male voice, lower than the alto, but higher than bass.

tenuto (teh-NOO-toh) [It.] Stress and extend the marked note.

text Words, usually set in a poetic style, that express a central thought, idea, moral, or narrative.

texture The thickness of the different layers of horizontal and vertical sounds.

theme and variation form A musical form in which variations of the basic theme comprise the composition.

tie A curved line connecting two successive notes of the same pitch, indicating that the second note is not to be articulated.

timbre Tone color; the unique quality produced by a voice or instrument.

time signature The sign placed at the beginning and within a composition to indicate the meter; for example, 4/4, 3/4; *see also* cut time, meter signature.

to coda Skip to the ⊕ or CODA.

tonality The organized relationships of pitches with reference to a definite key center. In Western music, most tonalities are organized by the major and minor scales.

tone A sound quality of a definite pitch.

tone color, quality, or timbre That which distinguishes the voice or tone of one singer or instrument from another; for example, a soprano from an alto or a flute from a clarinet.

tonic chord (TAH-nik kord) [Gk.] The name of a chord built on the tonal center of a scale; for example, C E G or *do*, *mi*, *so* for C major.

tonic or tonal center The most important pitch in a scale; *do*; the home tone; the tonal center or root of a key or scale.

tonic triad A three-note chord comprising root, third, and fifth; for example, C E G.

transposition The process of changing the key of a composition.

treble clef The symbol that appears at the beginning of the staff used for higher voices, instruments, or the piano right hand; generally referring to pitches above middle C, it wraps around the line for G, therefore it is also called the G-clef.

triad A three-note chord built in thirds above a root tone.

trill A rapid change between the marked note and the one above it within the same key.

triplet A group of notes in which three notes of equal duration are sung in the time normally given to two notes of equal duration.

troppo (TROHP-oh) [It.] Too much; for example, *allegro non troppo*, not too fast.

troubadour A wandering minstrel of noble birth in southern France, Spain, and Italy during the eleventh to thirteenth centuries.

tuning The process of adjusting the tones of voices or instruments so they will sound the proper pitches.

tutti (TOO-tee) [It.] Meaning "all" or "together."

twelve-tone music Twentieth-century system of writing music in which the twelve tones of the chromatic scale are arranged into a tone row (numbered 1 to 12), and then the piece is composed by arranging and rearranging the "row" in different ways; for example, backward, forward, or in clusters of three or four pitches.

U

unison Voice parts or instruments sounding the same pitches in the same rhythm simultaneously.

upbeat A weak beat preceding the downbeat.

V

variation *See* theme and variation form, musical variations.

vivace (vee-VAH-chay) [It.] Very fast; lively.

voice crossing (or voice exchange) When one voice "crosses" above or below another voice part.

W

whole step The combination of two successive half steps.

whole tone scale A scale consisting only of whole steps.

For use with Sight-Singing exercises. Use the keyboard and notation on this page to identify and perform the notes in your voice part.

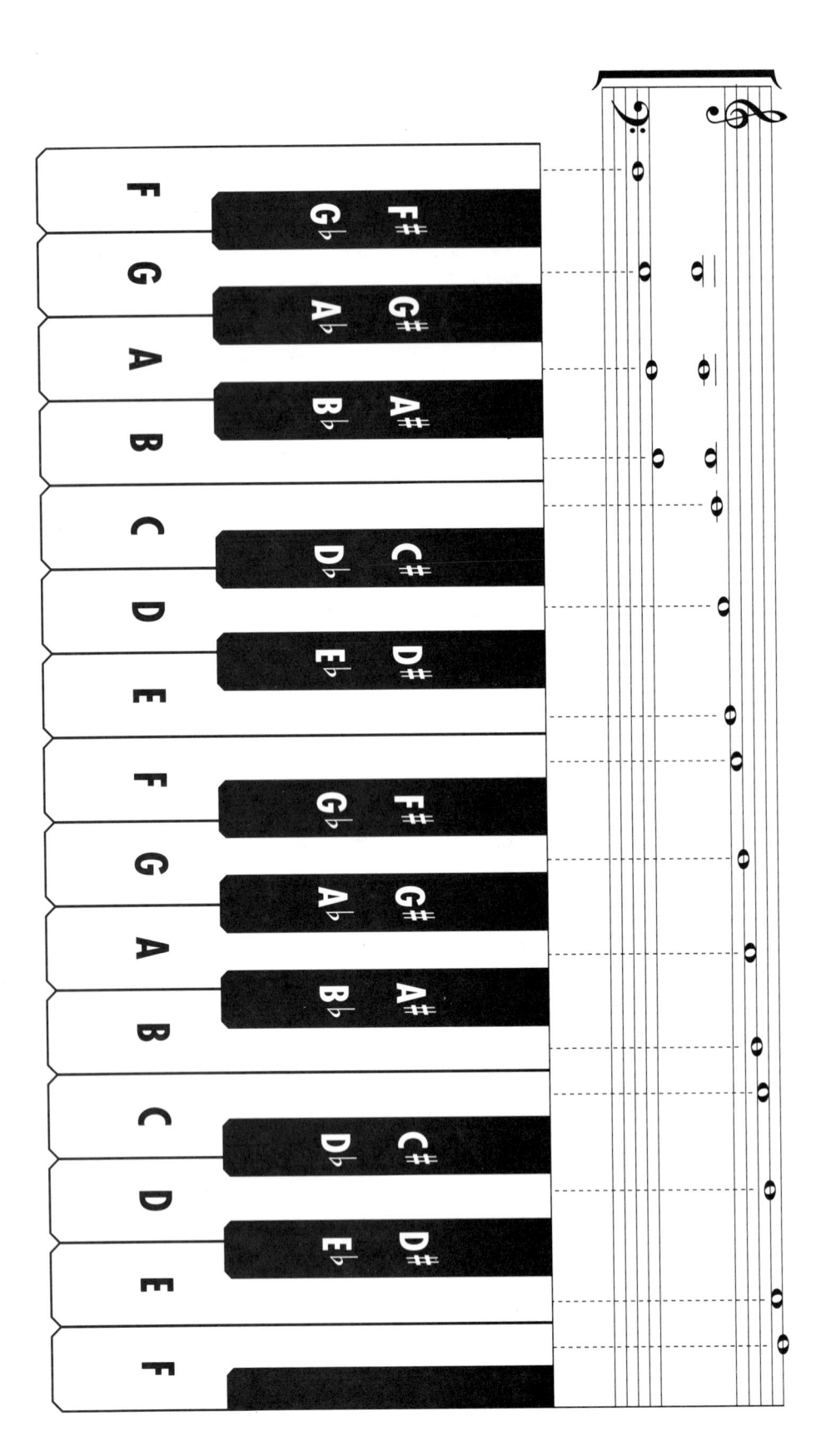